THIRD-DEGREE
GREEN BELT
SUDOKU®

FRANK LONGO

MARTIAL ARTS SUDOKU

GREEN

★ ★

NOT-SO-EASY®

P

**PUZZLE
WRIGHT
PRESS**

An imprint of Sterling
Publishing Co., Inc.

www.puzzlewright.com

CONTENTS

Introduction
3

Puzzles
5

Answers
155

Puzzlewright Press and the distinctive Puzzlewright Press logo are trademarks of
Sterling Publishing Co., Inc.

2   4   6   8   10   9   7   5   3   1

Published by Sterling Publishing Co., Inc.
387 Park Avenue South, New York, NY 10016
© 2009 by Sterling Publishing Co., Inc.
Distributed in Canada by Sterling Publishing
C/o Canadian Manda Group, 165 Dufferin Street
Toronto, Ontario, Canada M6K 3H6
Distributed in the United Kingdom by GMC Distribution Services
Castle Place, 166 High Street, Lewes, East Sussex, England BN7 1XU
Distributed in Australia by Capricorn Link (Australia) Pty. Ltd.
P.O. Box 704, Windsor, NSW 2756, Australia

Sterling ISBN 978-1-4027-4647-5

For information about custom editions, special sales, premium and
corporate purchases, please contact Sterling Special Sales
Department at 800-805-5489 or specialsales@sterlingpublishing.com.

INTRODUCTION

To solve sudoku puzzles, all you need to know is this one simple rule:

Fill in the boxes so that the nine rows, the nine columns, and the nine 3×3 sections all contain every digit from 1 to 9.

And that's all there is to it! Using this simple rule, let's see how far we get on this sample puzzle at right. (The letters at the top and left edges of the puzzle are for reference only; you won't see them in the regular puzzles.)

	A	B	C	D	E	F	G	H	I
J									
K					2		1	8	4
L	9		5		7		2		6
M	1		4	3	9	2		7	
N					7		6		
O		7		1	4	8	9		2
P	3		2		6		8		5
Q	8	4	9		3				
R									

The first number that can be filled in is an obvious one: box EN is the only blank box in the center 3×3 section, and all the digits 1 through 9 are represented except for 5. EN must be 5.

The next box is a little trickier to discover. Consider the upper left 3×3 section of the puzzle. Where can a 4 go? It can't go in AK, BK, or CK because row K already has a 4 at IK. It can't go in BJ or BL because column B already has a 4 at BQ. It can't go in CJ because column C already has a 4 at CM. So it must go in AJ.

Another box in that same section that can now be filled is BJ. A 2 can't go in AK, BK, or CK due to the 2 at EK. The 2 at GL rules out a 2 at BL. And the 2 at CP means that a 2 can't go in CJ. So BJ must contain the 2. It is worth noting that this 2 couldn't have been placed without the 4 at AJ in place.

Many of the puzzles rely on this type of steppingstone behavior.

We now have a grid as shown.

Let's examine column A. There are four blank boxes in column A; in which blank box must the 2 be placed? It can't be AK because of the 2 in EK (and the 2 in BJ). It can't be AO because of the 2 in IO. It can't be AR because of the 2 in CP. Thus, it must be AN that has the 2.

	A	B	C	D	E	F	G	H	I
J	4	2							
K					2		1	8	4
L	9		5		7		2		6
M	1		4	3	9	2		7	
N					7	5	6		
O		7		1	4	8	9		2
P	3		2		6		8		5
Q	8	4	9		3				
R									

By the 9's in AL, EM, and CQ, box BN must be 9. Do you see how?

We can now determine the value for box IM. Looking at row M and then column I, we find all the digits 1 through 9 are represented but 8. IM must be 8.

This brief example of some of the techniques leaves us with the grid at right.

You should now be able to use what you learned to fill in CN followed by BL, then HL followed by DL and FL.

As you keep going through this puzzle, you'll find it gets easier as you fill in more. And as you keep working through the puzzles in

	A	B	C	D	E	F	G	H	I
J	4	2							
K					2		1	8	4
L	9		5		7		2		6
M	1		4	3	9	2		7	8
N	2	9		7	5	6			
O		7		1	4	8	9		2
P	3		2		6		8		5
Q	8	4	9		3				
R									

this book, you'll find it gets easier and more fun each time. The final answer is shown below.

This book consists of 300 puzzles of medium level of difficulty.

—Frank Longo

	A	B	C	D	E	F	G	H	I
J	4	2	1	6	8	3	5	9	7
K	7	3	6	5	2	9	1	8	4
L	9	8	5	4	7	1	2	3	6
M	1	5	4	3	9	2	6	7	8
N	2	9	8	7	5	6	4	1	3
O	6	7	3	1	4	8	9	5	2
P	3	1	2	9	6	7	8	4	5
Q	8	4	9	2	3	5	7	6	1
R	5	6	7	8	1	4	3	2	9

1

9					3	7		4
	3			4				
		7				5		3
	9				1	3	6	
				8				
	1	6	7				2	
7		9				1		
				7			4	
8		1	9					6

2

		6		8				9
2							1	
	8		5		1			6
	5	8			9		6	
	3		6			7	8	
7			1		5		4	
	9							3
5				7		6		

					1			5
	5			2	8			
	8					3	2	4
5		3	9		2			6
6			7		3	2		8
3	6	9					5	
			6	9			8	
1			2					

	6							
					4		9	7
9		2	1		5			
	9			1		4		
8			5	4	7			3
		3		6			7	
			9		1	2		8
1	3		2					
							6	

5

		6						8
		8	4			7		
9	4		8					
	6		2					4
	8	7		4		9	3	
4					8		6	
					9		5	3
		9			3	2		
5						1		

6

				8		4	6	
	8		7					1
	3	1						2
			3	5		6		
	6						3	
		8		4	6			
5						2	4	
9					3		5	
	2	4		9				

7

3		6		5				
							3	8
1	8	5			7			
			3	4		8		
7	1						5	3
		3		8	5			
			4			6	9	5
6	2							
				9		3		7

8

	6			1			9	
8	9				4	5	7	
				7		1	6	
3				8				
			1		5			
			4					5
	4	5	7					
	1	2	4				5	9
	3		6			2		

9

				9			1	
	9	1		3		2		
3	6				1	5		
			7			1		
2		7				4		6
		8			9			
		3	9				4	8
		4		6		7	5	
	8			1				

1 0

	5	3			7			
8		9		6				
2			1					4
	7	4	5					
			3		9			
					2	4	9	
1					6			9
				1		7		8
			4			2	6	

			8	7				9
	2		4					8
	8						2	4
1				9		3	6	7
7	5	9		8				1
6	9						7	
2					4		5	
8				5	7			

			7					8
9						6	1	
	1	5						7
4			5	3			7	
8			1		4			9
	7			9	6			2
1						3	2	
	4	6						1
3					1			

2			5	4				
5					3		8	7
	9			8				1
	7						6	
1	2			9			7	3
	4						2	
4				6			1	
6	1		3					8
				7	9			6

	3	4	7	9				
			3	6				7
6	5				8			
	7	1						
		2	1		3	9		
						2	1	
			6				4	2
7				5	4			
				2	7	6	5	

15

7		2		3			9	
			1			4	7	
		9		8				1
		6	4			9		
	2						3	
		3			1	8		
8				1		7		
	3	7			6			
	6			5		1		3

16

	1	3						
							5	7
9			2	7		4		
2		1	9		3	8	7	
				5				
	7	5	1		2	6		3
		4		2	5			1
1	6							
						3	8	

Puzzle 17

								5
3	4				1	6		
7	1	9	6					
	2					8	9	4
				6				
9	7	4					1	
					5	7	6	1
		3	9				2	8
2								

Puzzle 18

	5	8		9				2
		7			4	9		
			6				3	
	8		5			3		
	3						4	
		2			3		7	
	7				9			
		4	1			6		
2				6		5	8	

			4	7		9	2	
2		7						8
			2	9				6
6					2	1		
	4						6	
		3	9					7
9			8	4				
5						6		1
	6	8		1	7			

				9	4			
2		7		5	8	4		
8		4						
1			8	4	7	3		
	4						7	
		8	1	6	2			4
						7		3
		3	6	7		1		2
			9	8				

2 1

		6				8	1	9
	9	4						
					6			
8			2		5			6
4		5	1		8	2		7
6			7		4			3
			3					
						3	7	
1	5	3				6		

2 2

							2	5
	9	7					6	
8					9			
4		8	2	7				
		3		4		6		
				5	1	8		4
			5					7
	4					1	3	
3	7							

		3	4	7			2	8
				2		9		
					9		4	
				3	1			2
2			5		8			7
6			7	9				
	7		1					
		5		8				
8	1			5	4	6		

5				9		7		
					4			
				7		8		3
	3		9				5	2
		5		6		1		
8	9				1		6	
6		2		3				
			6					
		3		5				1

2 / 5

		2						7
4					1			5
		7	6	9	3			
			2				4	
	2		1	4	5		6	
	7				6			
			9	6	2	4		
1			4					3
2						8		

2 / 6

					3		1	6
		4	6		1			7
			8			5	9	
1		9						5
	8	2				6	7	
6						9		8
	3	6			5			
2			9		6	7		
7	9		3					

9	3		5					1
	4	1		9				8
				7			3	
	2	9			7			
				3				
			9			5	4	
	9			4				
8				6		1	7	
3					8		2	4

9				8		5		7
8			4					
		4	9		6			3
	1	9			8	7		
	7						3	
		2	5			6	1	
5			2		4	8		
					9			2
2		7		5				9

6			7	5				4
	9							5
		7					2	
7	2				4		1	
		5		3		9		
	4		6				7	2
	1					4		
4							8	
3				8	6			1

	6						9	
			4					8
5			3	2			4	
6				8		5	7	
9				6				4
	2	4		9				3
	5			3	7			1
7					2			
	9						3	

		8	1				7	
3	9	2		5				
6				8		3		
		6						
	1	5	2		6	7	3	
						4		
		7		4				2
				2		1	6	7
	6				1	5		

1				7		8		3
		6						
9	5	8					4	
	4			9				
		1	3	6	8	4		
				2			3	
	3					2	7	1
						9		
7		2		4				8

2		7	9		4			
	6			7			2	
4				8		5		
1		4						
	3		7		8		4	
						6		8
		8		5				3
	2			3			8	
			8		9	7		6

		6	3	1			5	
5		1		8				
3						6		
	9	8	2					
		5				1		
				4	5	3		
		9						2
				2		8		7
	2			6	9	3		

Puzzle 1:

			1	3	5		4	
		5			4		3	
					9			
					3			6
3			6	9	8			2
8			7					
		2						
	1		3			8		
	5		2	7	9			

Puzzle 2:

		3		5		2		
		2	6				3	4
7	1				4		5	
					3	5		
		8	2					
	5		9				1	8
4	9				1	6		
		1		7		4		

3/7

					5		1	
3	7			1		2		8
6	2					9		
	8		5					
1				4				2
					1		7	
		3					6	4
4		9		7			2	3
	5		3					

3/8

8	5	1		3	2			
7		6		9		8	5	
2		5						
	7		6		1		2	
						7		9
	8	2		5		4		7
			2	7		9	8	3

6			2			5	9	
	5	8		4				3
								6
		2		8	1		3	
	6						7	
	3		4	2		9		
1								
4				9		2	1	
	8	5			4			9

		3			2		6	7
7		4			6	9		2
9				8		3		
			2	6				
5								6
				9	1			
		8		2				5
3		9	6			8		1
1	7		4			6		

		5		3			4	
1		2						7
	9	7	2					
								8
7			6	1	4			3
5								
					5	4	6	
3						1		9
	4			9		8		

	3	6		5			1	
								9
	1	8	9	6		7		2
7					5			
		9				1		
			7					4
2		1		3	4	9	7	
3								
	7			2		8	4	

3					9		6	
	5		7			8		
	7	4						
7			8	3				9
5	8						3	1
4				1	7			5
						9	1	
		3			6		5	
	1		2					6

							7	
		4				5		6
2	9	5						
	8			1	4			
1	2		5	7	6		9	8
			2	9		5		
						3	1	7
6		8				9		
	7							

	7		5	8		2		
								7
2					7	6		5
3		2	8			5		
	1			7			2	
		5			1	8		9
4		7	3					2
9								
		1		4	8		5	

			8	5			3	
8		3			6		4	
7	5				3			
						4		2
6		1				3		7
9		7						
			4				2	3
	7		3			1		5
	9			6	2			

27

			7					
	4			5	8	1		3
		3				6	7	9
		8						2
4			3		5			8
2						7		
7	8	2				3		
3		6	1	7			4	
					3			

9		8				1		
					7		6	
			8			5	3	
3		2		5	6			
			4		8			
			7	2		6		1
	7	6			2			
	2		5					
		4				9		5

	9	3						8
	8		1	6	3			7
3				2			7	
4	7		3		5		2	9
	5			9				1
8			7	5	2		1	
5						7	8	

	8			9	7			5
	7	9						
2		6		1			8	
			5			9		
5	9						1	7
		3			9			
	2			7		4		1
						5	2	
1			9	4			7	

	5	7						
				7				6
	8	4		9	2	7		1
	6		7				4	
			9		3			
	9				6		7	
9		5	4	6		1	2	
2				1				
						4	8	

			2					8
3					5		9	
	2		3		4		1	
7	9	3						4
				4				
6						7	8	1
	6		9		2		7	
	7		8					3
1					6			

						2	6	
		3	2		5			1
2	1		9					
			1		3			5
6	5						4	3
7			5		6			
					8		9	2
1			3		9	7		
	2	6						

	2	8		5	6			9
		6	2			4		
	1							6
				2				1
		1		6		9		
2				9				
1							7	
		3			5	2		
8			9	3		1	4	

Puzzle 1:

		1		4	2			
5						3		8
					1		9	
			8		7	9	2	
		2	9		4	5		
	8	5	6		3			
	7		1					
3		6						2
			2	6		7		

Puzzle 2:

	9	8					4	
3			5			8		
		5	4					
2	4		9	5				
9		6		3		2		5
				2	7		9	8
					1	9		
		1			5			6
	3					1	8	

				4		8	1	
			2		7	5		
2								
	3	1	9		8			5
		2				3		
7			1		4	2	8	
								6
		9	3		2			
	8	5		6				

5					1			
4	9	3		6				
			4	7		3		
		6				9	5	
	5		8		6		3	
	2	9				1		
		2		1	7			
				5		6	9	8
			9					2

	3	6	4				7	2
	5	1		2				
		8			6			
				4		3		
		3	5		2	9		
	1		7					
			1			2		
				4		6	8	
1	6				3	5	4	

				9				6
2	3				6			
6			2			5	3	4
	7	2	4			8		3
9		3			8	1	5	
3	1	4			5			8
			3				2	1
7				6				

		2			8			7
		4	9			6		
	5			4				
			8		6	2		5
		5		9		3		
6		9	1		3			
				8			4	
		6			9	8		
3			4			9		

1				5				
		2	1			8		4
6			2		8			5
	1		6	8		7		
		6		9	3		2	
4			9		2			7
5		7			4	2		
				6				3

6
3

5		4					8	
	8				1		5	
			5				7	9
3		5						
9	1			7			4	3
						1		2
1	5				2			
	6		8				2	
	3					9		4

6
4

1	5	8						
		7			1			4
			8			5		
	9		2	5	8			
3								5
		5	7	3			4	
	3		9					
7			8			4		
						2	9	6

65

3	8							5
					1		6	8
6				2			3	
		9			3		7	
2			6		8			4
	3		4			6		
	1			6				3
8	7		5					
5							4	6

66

	9	6	7					
		3	8		4			
							8	7
9			6	7				4
7				8				5
2				3	9			1
5	2							
			2			3	7	
						7	1	2

		8				4		9
				4				8
4		9		8	3			
					2			3
1		6				5		4
8			6					
			4	9		6		2
9				5				
3		1				9		

9			1		5	4	6	
		1						
	3		4	9				5
4					2	9	1	
				8				
	7	9	5					3
3				4	8		5	
						8		
	8	5	2		1			4

	1	8						
		5	8	4		3		9
							7	8
		2	6		4	1		
	5			9			8	
		1	2		8	9		
5	3							
1		4		3	7	2		
						4	3	

						5		7
	2			1		9		3
	5		7	6				
					1	2		
2				7				8
		1	3					
			8	6			4	
9		8		2			1	
3		6						

Puzzle 7/1

		9		6		5		
3	8						6	
4			8	2				
		8		5				
2	4						5	1
			1			9		
			4	6				3
	7						1	2
		2		9		8		

Puzzle 7/2

5		4				8	1	
				1				2
		2					9	
	6			3	4			
9		1	6		8	4		3
			1	5			6	
	5					2		
2				7				
		3	7			9		6

9			7				8	
	7		9	3				4
3					4		6	9
								1
			3	8	7			
4								
7	4		2					6
6				7	5		2	
	9		8		6			3

		5		4	8			
4			2		6			8
9						5		
	5			6	1	2		7
			4		5			
1		9	7	3			5	
		2						5
7			5		3			6
			6	2		1		

7/5

	4			3	6			9
8		9					1	3
			9					4
1						5	8	
			2		3			
	2	5						7
5					4			
9	8					7		6
4			7	6			3	

7/6

	7	8	5	4		9		3
	9						8	
					1			4
7					8			5
				5				
2			3					9
9			8					
	5						2	
8		4		1	5	7	9	

	8		6					
5	2				9		8	
6						1		3
		5	2	4		8		
				1				
		9		6	5	4		
3		2						6
	5		1				4	9
					6		3	

8					1			7
			4		3	1		
4	2							3
			3	6	7		4	
6								8
	3		8	2	4			
9							6	4
		2	6		9			
7			1					2

					7		4	9
	5	7		2		8		6
		9	4					
			3	4		9		
		8				4		
	9		7	5				
					2	1		
9		5		8		2	7	
1	7		5					

6		3			8			
9			6		5	3		
2	7							
1	5			9		4		
				7				
		7		8			3	1
							9	2
		1	8		2			3
			3			8		6

Puzzle 8/1

6		7		5				
		8						9
				6		5	3	
5					4		8	1
		4		3		7		
8	7		9					2
	2	1		9				
3						6		
				4		9		5

Puzzle 8/2

	9			4				6
			9			5		8
			3	2	6	4	9	
9	1					8		
		7					6	5
	5	8	2	1	4			
6		1			7			
2				3			5	

	1							
3		7	1			4		
		6		9	5	3		8
2					3	9		
			8		9			
		9	6					3
1		4	3	6		8		
		8			2	5		6
							7	

4					2	1		5
		6			9			
2		8		1			3	
				6		7		
	2		1		3		4	
		1		2				
	1			9		3		8
			2			4		
8		2	5					1

2	6				1			
5				9			7	4
	9	4		8				
			5					
	2	6		7		9	1	
					6			
				3		8	6	
6	7			1				3
			8				4	2

9	6			1	8			5
						3		8
			5			9	6	7
			6				2	9
5	1		4					
2	3	1	9					
4		5						
6			5	3			8	2

87

			5			7		
	3			8			6	
		1		3			8	
6			4	1			3	
		4				9		
	8			2	6			7
	1			9		2		
	5			4			1	
		9			8			

88

	8	9					7	
	2		1	6				8
7		6	5	8				
						6		
3		1				5		4
		5						
			1	2		7		3
6			3	5			2	
	3					8	6	

8			5				7	
	6	4		1	7			8
		7				1		
	8			2		4		1
				6				
1		3		5			8	
		8				6		
4			6	7		5	3	
	3				5			9

2				5		4		6
	6				8		1	
	3		7					
		3			2	7	5	
5								8
	7	1	8			9		
					9		7	
	1		2				9	
3		8		7				2

7				8	3		2	
9	5					6		
4					6			
					1	9		2
		2				3		
1		4	2					
			7					8
		6					1	9
	8		3	1				5

	5			8	2		1	6
			1			5		
6			5	3				8
5								
	1	4				2	3	
								7
7				4	8			2
		6			5			
9	4		6	2			7	

				4	5		9	2
		7	1			8		3
			3					
		6	9			5		4
	9			2			8	
8		3			7	9		
					8			
3		4			9	2		
2	5		7	3				

6								
1	8	7	6				4	
	3		2		4			
5	9					8		
		8	5	7	2	4		
		6					5	1
			7		5		1	
	2				9	5	6	4
								9

Puzzle 9/5

3					4	7		
4	7						5	6
		5						
		1		5	9		6	
9								1
	6		7	1		4		
						1		
2	8						9	5
		7	2					8

Puzzle 9/6

		9		1				
		9		1				
				5		6		8
	5		7	3				4
2					1			
		1		6		9		
			3					5
1			8	3		2		
6		8	9					
			7		5			

				4	3		5	2
				6	5		1	
1							7	
		2		5		6	4	1
7	6	4		1		8		
	7							3
	9		6	7				
5	2		9	3				

						1	9	6
							2	4
3	1	9			6			
4				6	2			
	2			5			4	
			1	3				7
			9			7	3	1
8	9							
1	4	3						

				8	5			2
			6		9		5	
						6	9	1
4			2			1	6	8
6	2	8			1			9
9	3	5						
	1		4		3			
7			1	9				

8		1			2		4	
				3			9	
7	9		6				2	
				6				4
	7		8		9		6	
2				1				
	2				4		7	6
	1			8				
	4		5			8		2

3			4				9	
					6	5		7
		4		7				
4		2	6				5	
8			1		5			9
	5				7	8		4
				2		3		
7		5	3					
	8				4			5

				2	7	9		
	8	7		1				
		1	6		9			3
		8	9					2
				5				
1					6	4		
8			5		3	7		
				7		5	2	
		6	2	9				

103

	1				2			
4			9					
				7	4	5		
3			1			7		2
7				8				6
5		8			9			1
		2	6	3				
					5			7
			8				6	

104

			2				3	
7			4					6
1	3		9			5		
8	9					3		
		7					9	8
		2			8		1	7
4					5			3
	7				3			

1			7	2				
	2	9						8
		8	5	6			2	
			1		4			6
	5						4	
4			2		6			
	6			7	2	4		
5						6	7	
				3	5			9

				5			6	2
1		5			6			8
						9		
5			8	7			1	
	7			9			8	
	8			6	2			3
		7						
3			1			4		6
8	2			3				

8	1				9	7		
		6					5	
	9		6					
	3		7	6				2
		8		9		1		
2				1	3		4	
					6		8	
	2					4		
		7	5				6	1

			6			9		
	7	2					3	6
6		3					4	5
			3	9				2
		6	8		4	7		
3				2	6			
5	3					6		9
9	2					5	7	
		1			5			

7		2	4		3		9	
3		6	2					
	9			5			8	
5	7	8						
						5	1	7
	4			1			2	
					9	3		1
	3		7		5	4		8

	8	7				4	6	
6	9	4		8				1
			8		7			9
		8		4		7		
2			3		5			
7				1		3	9	4
	3	6				2	7	

1				3	8		6	5
	6				5		4	
7					9			
		2					7	
3				4				8
	5					9		
			3					4
	3		7				2	
6	4		5	9				7

		5			1			
	2	4	8					
1	3	6	2					
7					5		6	
6								2
	8		6					3
					3	7	4	6
					9	3	2	
			7			9		

1 1 3

9	6					8		2
	2		1				9	
								3
	9	4	3	1				8
3				4				6
1				2	5	3	4	
2								
	4				2		3	
8		1					7	5

1 1 4

6	3	5	2					3
6	3	5		1	9			
			5			9		
	1		8	5				7
		9				8		
4				9	7		2	
		1			5			
			7	2		3	4	1
3					1			

	6				1	4			3
		3	9	8					1
	4								
		5			6				
	3		4	2	1			8	
			3			9			
								2	
5				7	3	8			
3			5	6				1	

					9			5
7							1	
5			3		1	4	2	
9			2		8			
		1				8		
			5		6			4
	5	3	6		4			7
	7							2
2			9					

6				2				
			6		8	2		
2		4	1				5	
	3	2				5		
1		7				8		2
		9				4	1	
	4				1	7		3
		8	4		2			
				5				4

2				5				6
1								
	8	5	4		9			
	5	2	6		3	8		4
8		6	9		2	7	5	
			5		1	9	4	
								2
7				3				5

119

1		3	9					
6			5				2	
2				3	7			
9		4				1		
	2						6	
		5				4		9
			7	5				6
	7				2			1
					9	5		4

120

			8		5	7		
3			4	6				8
	9			4				
	7				4	8	9	
	1	5	7				2	
				3			6	
8					6	3		5
		1	5		7			

	1				7			8
		7	5				9	
4				2		7	5	
						8		
7	2		9		8		6	3
		5						
	5	2		9				4
	4				1	6		
8			4				2	

		3	7				9	
6	5			4	9			2
4			1			6		
9	8						1	
	7						4	6
		9			1			4
2			5	9			3	1
	3				7	9		

Puzzle 1 (1 2 3)

			9	1			6	
		5						
	7		3		6		9	
1				7				8
5	3		6		4		7	9
7				3				5
	6		8		1		2	
						7		
	5			6	3			

Puzzle 2 (1 2 4)

			4		2			3
	5						4	
7		3				8		
					7	5		9
		2	8		9	3		
5		1	3					
		7				2		1
	2						3	
4			6		1			

	4	8		3				
	5					7		3
7		2					8	
8					4	5		
		4		1		2		
		3	5					6
	7					6		4
2		9					7	
				5		3	2	

		3			6			
5				1	9	8		
		2						4
6		1	2		4			5
4				3				1
3			5		1	9		8
1						5		
		4	8	9				7
			1			4		

7	1		4	3	9			
	5	8			1	4		
9					7			
	4	1						
8								9
						1	6	
			9					1
		6	8			9	4	
			7	6	4		3	8

				4				
4			2	8		5		
						4	1	
	7	1	4				8	9
			5		7			
9	4				3	7	2	
	3	2						
	1		3	5				6
			8					

129

8			3		7	1	4	
	1				2		5	
	7						9	3
			6	2		5		
		1		3	8			
4	3						8	
	9		4				2	
	2	6	9		5			1

130

			1					6
	4		8				2	
	3			4	9	5		1
		8						
	5	7				8	3	
						9		
7		3	9	8			6	
	8				4		9	
9					5			

1 3 1

	5	4	3	8			1	
1		6			7			
							5	7
		8		5			3	6
6	3			9		7		
3	7							
			6			5		1
	6				1	4	2	7

1 3 2

					4		3	2
6			9	3				
	8			1		9		
	5	1		2				
	4						6	
				9		2	8	
		9		4			7	
				8	1			5
3	1		7					

4	5				6			
	1			8			3	
6					9			8
		1		3			8	6
2								7
8	4			5		3		
9			5					3
	2			1			7	
			2				6	4

6	8			4			9	
	3	1	9					
2					7	1		
			1	5			2	
		2				8		
	5			7	4			
		3	4					9
				3	7	1		
	1			2			8	4

Puzzle 1

1					7		3	
		3		2				
			8		1			9
7		6				1		8
				6				
8		2				9		6
6			2		3			
				9		4		
	9		4					7

Puzzle 2

		7			1	9		
		9		3				
3					2			5
6				4	7			
1		5				3		8
			5	1				2
8			7					4
				2		5		
		1	6			2		

Puzzle 137

					4		7	
			5			6		
7	3	4	8					
		5	6		3	7		
1		3		4		2		8
		7	2		1	3		
					8	9	3	6
		1			7			
	6		3					

Puzzle 138

5		8			2	3		7
	9	7			8			
2		6		1				
		2			5			
	6			8			5	
			2			1		
				5		6		1
			4			5	9	
1		5	6			7		3

9							7	
4				7	2			
7	1					5	4	
			5	4	6		9	
	5		9	8	3			
	7	9					8	3
			8	9				5
	2							1

		4						1
					2			5
3	7	5	6					
					7	3	5	4
			9		6			
4	2	1	8					
					3	6	1	9
8			7					
1					8			

	7				3			6
3				7				
9	8				1			
		5	2				9	
	4		3		9		6	
	6				4	1		
			5				3	9
				3				8
8			9				7	

	2	4				5		7
		8					6	
1	6				5			
8		1	2					
			3	9	7			
					1	4		2
			5				9	6
	5					3		
6		7				8	5	

9				3		8		6
			7		1			4
	5						1	
		6			8	7		
	9						4	
		2	9			3		
	3						6	
8			6		2			
1		7		9				2

		8			9			
9				1	4	7		
1	4							
	3		9			6		4
6	9						3	8
4		7			8		9	
							6	7
		9	7	6				1
			2			9		

145

	6	2		9	8		1	
					3	8		
3	4			2				
						6		1
5								2
4		7						
				1			9	3
		5	3					
	9		6	4		1	8	

146

				2				5
		8	9		5		1	
			6					3
	4			6	2			9
6	3		4		1		2	8
5			7	9			4	
4					6			
	2		8		9	4		
1				4				

	1		3					7
	5	6	9				3	
7	3			8			9	5
	4			9				
			2		4			
				3			1	
8	6			1			4	9
	9				6	8	5	
1					9		7	

	3	8	7	9				
					3	9		
1	7							3
		3			7	1		4
4								8
7		5	9			3		
8							2	1
		7	6					
				5	2	7	3	

7					3	1	9	
	2	9		8	5		6	
								5
			5				8	
		6		3		4		
	3				2			
6								
	8		9	1		3	4	
	9	4	3					8

	1					2		8
			9			4		7
4			8	1		3		
6				4		9	2	
	8	1		9				5
		8	1	6				4
1		3			7			
9		4					6	

Puzzle 1:

	9			4				1
	7	8	1	9				
	5	1			6	4		
9		6			5			
			3			2		6
		8	9			1	5	
			6	3	1	7		
7				5			9	

Puzzle 2:

2		8				9		
1					8	3		
4			9		2			
		4			3	6		
3				6				8
		5	7			4		
			8		4			5
		7	1					4
		3				7		6

		7		8		6		
3								
2	6			1	9			
7				2	8	3	9	
	5	8	3	7				1
			2	6			5	7
								2
		2		4		9		

					4		2	
					1	5		
			2		8	6	3	4
5	3					2	7	
			4		3			
	1	2					4	8
6	2	9	1		5			
		7	9					
	5		3					

	3		6					
4							5	
		9			4	3	8	2
				8		1		5
		8	4	3	1	7		
2		7		6				
1	8	3	2			9		
	4							7
					6		1	

1					6		5	2
	2				7			
3			4				1	
8		7						
4		3		5		2		6
						9		8
	8				3			9
			5				8	
6	4		7					5

157

					8		4	7
3								
8			7		1	5		3
			8		4	3		5
				6				
7		6	2		5			
5		7	4		9			1
								2
2	1		5					

158

			2	1		7		
	7	4	5					
3		5						1
				7		1		6
	3						5	
4		6		3				
7						4		9
					8	2	1	
		3		9	4			

			5	4	7			6
								9
1		2			3	4	7	
7			8					2
	2						6	
5					9			7
	1	5	2			6		8
2								
6			3	5	1			

		6			2	4	1	
9	8			1				
		4						
				3		5	4	
	2		7		8		9	
	4	9		6				
						6		
				7			8	5
	9	3	4			7		

					7			
3		6		4	2	8		
	9						6	2
				2		1		
5		8	4		1	2		9
		1		5				
8	1						3	
		3	1	7		5		6
			8					

	7	2						
4		5	2					
	8				6			3
3						2		
	4		3	7	8		1	
		9						4
5			9				8	
					5	1		6
						7	4	

Puzzle 163

8						3		4
			3		2		9	
					9		7	1
5						6	2	
			4		8			
	2	9						3
4	5		2					
	8		6		3			
2		7						8

Puzzle 164

			1				6	
2	8			9		3		1
		7		2			8	
	3				9			6
4				3				5
8			5				2	
	2			7		6		
1		9		6			3	7
	7				1			

165

		3	2			9	7	
	4		3	9				
2			7					6
9	1							
5				3				8
							9	7
4					5			9
				2	3		4	
	9	2			8	5		

166

			2					
	8							7
7	2						1	3
3		7	5	8				1
	5			6			8	
8				7	4	6		5
9	7						5	8
4							2	
					9			

9	4							3
	2				3		7	
				7		1		2
6		3		1		9		
	1						3	
		2		9		5		6
5		6		3				
	3		7				6	
8							5	1

	3		2		6	4		
			5		4		7	
		7					8	
					1	3		2
				2				
5		1	6					
	7					1		
	1		3		9			
		6	7		8		3	

5					1		4	3
						6		
9	2		3			5		
			3	5	1			7
4								9
2		1	9	6				
		5			3		8	6
		8						
7	6		1					5

	3					6	2	
				8				
			6	1		4		3
9		1			5	3		
	2						7	
		8	2			1		9
7		9		5	3			
				7				
	6	5					9	

		3			9			1
		8		3			2	
		6	2			9		7
							6	9
6		1				3		4
7	3							
1		9			6	7		
	8			2		6		
2			8			1		

					8			
	1			4				8
9			1			3	7	4
8	7		3			5	1	2
1	3	5			2		4	7
7	4	3			1			9
6				5			3	
			8					

		3	7			2		
6	9		3	1			7	
4				5				
		4					5	
	5		1		2		3	
	3					9		
			8					5
	2		3	1			6	9
		7			5	1		

		4	7	9				
		8		4			9	
5							3	
		7			6		4	
4			5	1	2			7
	8		9			3		
	1							8
	6			3		2		
				5	7	9		

3		4			5		8	
5	1				6			
				3	1			
	7		2			5		
		8		9		6		
		2			7		4	
			7	1				
			6				5	9
	3		5			7		2

9		1		6			4	7
2			8					
	8			5	1			
6					5			
7	1						2	5
			7					1
			1	4			9	
					9			8
8	9			2		5		4

5	8				1	2	3	
	6		3	4				
				5			7	
7			6				9	
6								7
	3				7			1
	5			9				
				1	3		8	
	4	8	5				1	3

			7				3	
4		7	1	6				
				4	5	7		8
3					6	9		
	4						2	
		6	9					5
1		2	6	3				
				9	2	6		3
	9				4			

		1				4		
2	4				6			
		5		1	4			
	1		9	4				8
7				6				4
8				3	5		1	
			7	9		8		
			4				5	1
		2				7		

8			6	2				1
2	1				7		9	
	9	6						
	5		9	8				4
				6				
4				7	2		1	
						1	4	
	2		4				5	8
3				5	8			6

	7				1			8
		2		3				
1			8	9			7	
5					7	6		2
			2		6			
8		6	3					5
	9			2	5			7
				4		8		
4			9				2	

2						7		
1	5		6		7			
			1	2			5	
	3			4			8	1
		2				4		
4	6			1			3	
	4			3	6			
			5		2		6	4
		7						5

	8				2	4		1
	6			7			2	5
				1		7		
		9					5	
			2	4	9			
	7					2		
		4		9				
7	3			2			1	
2		1	6				8	

6						7		
	4			6				
			7			2	9	6
4	8		2					7
		7	1		6	4		
3				4			2	9
8	3	6			1			
				2			3	
		5						1

	5		3					9
					9	2	4	
		9	4					
	8	2			7	3	5	
6		5				9		4
	9	4	5			8	2	
					5	6		
	1	3	7					
5					2		3	

			5	9		1		
			4				3	
		5			7		2	
		4						1
		2	8		6	3		
8						9		
	7		6			5		
	4				2			
		6		4	3			

	4	1	9		6		7	
	9			4	7			
		6						1
							5	2
1	6						3	4
4	3							
3						5		
			7	8			4	
	2		5		3	9	6	

	9				1			
		8	3	4				
3	1		2					
4		6				7		
5			1		7			8
		3				9		5
					5		4	3
				8	3	5		
			7				1	

Puzzle 189

			9			3		
		8	7					
		5		4			8	1
	4							8
	8		4		3		1	
3							9	
6	2			8		1		
					6	2		
		7			1			

Puzzle 190

					5			7
9				3			8	
		8	6				3	
		6		5	8	9		
5								4
		1	9	2		8		
	5				1	6		
	1			4				3
3			5					

	3	2	6					4
	4			8				7
7		6						
			7	9				8
		7	2		8	9		
9				6	4			
						4		1
3				1			5	
4					7	2	3	

				5	3			
4		7	6				3	5
		5	7		9		6	
7			5					
		8		9		5		
					4			7
	2		9		5	7		
9	8				2	1		3
			3	6				

193

6				4	1			3
		7					1	
	1	3	8		7			4
			9					6
	7			1			3	
5					8			
1			2		5	3	6	
	9					1		
7			1	6				8

194

9								4
4	3				2			
			3			7		
3	4			8				
	8	9	6		4	5	1	
				5			4	2
		3			8			
			5				9	1
6								7

						7		5
				7				
3			2		6	9	1	
6					8	5	9	
		1				4		
	5	8	4					3
	3	4	7		9			1
				6				
9		6						

5			6		2		9	
				4				
2	9			7		5	4	
	5	1					7	2
9	3					8	1	
	4	2		5			8	6
				1				
	7		4		6			9

				7	2		4	
			3			8	6	
6			5					
	9		2					3
7		5				2		4
3					8		1	
					9			1
	1	7		4				
	3		1	2				

4		8			7			5
	5			9		4		
	7				4			
		3		5	6			9
	9			2			7	
7			9	8		6		
			6				2	
		5		4			8	
6			2			5		4

3		5				7		8
				8			2	
			5	2			1	
4			7				8	
			2		4			
	3				8			4
	5			9	2			
	6			1				
1		8				2		6

2	9		8	1			6	
	6		7					
4	1			9	2			
8						4		
9	4						1	2
		2						8
			2	8			7	6
					9		4	
	8			3	6		5	1

		8		9		4		7
		4	7					
7			1			8	3	
		1						6
			8	6	1			
3						7		
	1	7			9			3
					5	2		
4		9		3		5		

	5				9			
7		2			6		9	
			5			7		2
8	4				5			1
6			7				2	3
5		1			3			
	8		9				1	6
			6				8	

203

		9		5	1			
		5				6	8	
					7	1	5	
4							7	
9			4	7	6			3
	6							2
	7	3	6					
	8	6				4		
			2	8		7		

204

6	4		9	1				
			6	5			4	
5				4	2			6
						5	2	7
	3						1	
7	5	1						
2			3	8				5
	7			2	6			
				9	1		3	2

205

		3	2			7		
5					8		4	
	1				9			
8	3				5	6	2	
		6				1		
	9	1	6				8	5
			5				9	
	7		3					1
		9			7	5		

206

				6	7	2		
	3		8		1	5		
		1		4				
7			4				9	
1		4				8		2
	8				5			6
				3		6		
		2	1		6		8	
		8	2	5				

7		8	3					6
				1	7			2
	3						8	
4				7		6	5	
				5				
	5	7		8				4
	6						2	
5			6	3				
3					2	7		8

				7	6			9
		9					2	
4						5		6
		6	2	1		7		
	2	8				6	4	
		3		4	5	2		
2		5						7
	9					8		
3			7	5				

	5		8		2			9
	2		1					5
4		9	7			6		
6	7	5				8		
		4				1	2	6
		7			3	2		1
3					1		9	
5			9		6		7	

2		8				6		
3				4	1	2	8	
						5	7	
				7			5	
		3	9		5	1		
	8			6				
	3	2						
	1	4	7	8				5
		9				8		6

211

	8		3	7				2
6		3				1	9	
7				2				
						5	2	
		9	2		4	7		
	1	6						
				1				3
	5	2				9		1
1				3	8		7	

212

	3	2	4				1	
8						7		
		1		9			6	
		5			1	6		
1	6						2	7
		8	7			9		
	8			3		4		
		7						6
	1				5	8	9	

2 1 3

	2	7		9				
	5	8		1				
			2		8		4	
2	8		4			5		
		5			6		8	4
	3		6		9			
				4		3	7	
				7		4	9	

2 1 4

		7						4
					4	2	9	
			5	2			3	6
		8	4			1		9
7								2
3		5			9	6		
5	7			6	8			
	8	9	3					
1						9		

215

		3				4		
1								
8		5	6	1				3
		4	2			1		
5			7		6			8
		9			5	6		
9				3	8	5		2
								6
		7				3		

216

		6				2	5	
				6				4
2		4			9		8	
			2	9		7		
7				4				3
		2		8	3			
	5		1			4		2
9				5				
	1	7				3		

217

2		7	3					
		9		5			1	
	8	6	4					
7					4		3	5
				6				
4	3		2					9
					9	5	4	
	7			8		3		
					6	7		8

218

9	4	8	7				5	
	2	6			1			9
				9				
		7		3				2
		3				6		
4				7		9		
			4					
7			6			3	9	
	6				7	2	1	8

3			6					
	5	8		4	2			3
9				5				
						6	4	
		6	2		7	8		
	7	1						
				6				8
2			5	1		3	7	
					3			9

8							5	
2	6							
			2		5	6		1
		2	8	9				
4								7
			1	2	4			
7		4	5		9			
							7	3
	3							5

		3			8			
		7				8		6
				7			4	2
9					5			1
7	1		6		2		8	5
3			7					9
2	3			8				
8		9				2		
			9			5		

			6			4		
2	9	6				1		
				1			2	6
3					5			
	2	8	1	7	4	3	5	
			3					8
7	1			5				
		5				8	7	4
		2			3			

				1				7
	7				5		1	
		1	6	2		3		4
		2		4	8			
	8						7	
			9	5		1		
7		4		8	6	5		
	5		2				3	
2				3				

		9				4		
	8			2		5		3
4		2					6	8
3			1			8		
			6		5			
		8			3			5
8	9					2		4
7		5		9			8	
		1				6		

225

		1	6	8		9	2	
					7			
3		8		5	2	1		
	1	9		7			8	
	7			3		5	9	
		4	3	9		2		6
			7					
	6	7		2	4	3		

226

		6	7			5		
8	4			6		2		
	9		5			8		
			4	8				3
	6			9			4	
9				3	5			
		3			4		7	
		9		7			5	2
		2			6	3		

		2	8				6	
		6	5	9				
7								1
5	7		2			1		
		1			8		9	4
9								5
				2	4	8		
	8				3	2		

					4			
7	3				6		9	
		8		9		7		2
	5				2			
2	8						5	1
			4				6	
1		7		6		8		
	9		8				4	7
			3					

2
2
9

	7				8			
8		3	6					
4		5						1
7					2	5		
3	8		7		9		1	2
	2		8					7
2						1		9
				2		7		6
			6				2	

2
3
0

				2	9	8		
			8			3	6	
		8	3					
	6		1			4	3	
	1	5				9	7	
	2	4			6		1	
					7	6		
	9	2			3			
		3	9	8				

Puzzle 2 3 1

			6		5	8	7	
8		5						
	7		4			3		
3	1				4			
9								3
			3				2	5
		3			6		9	
						6		1
	2	6	5		1			

Puzzle 2 3 2

				2		8		9
	7		9				1	
				1		6		3
		7			1			5
6				5				8
8			6			4		
3		8		9				
	1				3		9	
7		9		6				

	2	6						
5			7	9			1	
		1			2	5		9
							9	7
		7		5		4		
2	8							
1		9	3			2		
	5			6	4			3
						6	7	

		9	8			5	4	
						8		
5	8			4				3
	9		6		7			4
3								6
4			9		2		3	
9				1			8	5
		7						
	5	3			9	6		

		7						5
9				5		6	3	
	8		9		3			
2		3	6					
			2	4	7			
					9	2		7
			3		1		6	
	1	6		8				3
4						8		

	3	7				4	9	
						7		
9			2	8				
1				5			3	8
				1				
5	2			4				7
				7	9			1
		9						
	6	2				9	5	

	8		3			2		
	4		1				5	
		2		8	7	1		3
8				3			1	
4								5
	7			9				6
9		8	5	1		7		
	5				8		3	
		7			3		8	

3	5	4	8					
		9				8		
	7		6	9	2			
						6	3	4
				1				
9	4	7						
			3	8	5		7	
		8				3		
					9	4	8	2

Puzzle 239

			7				9	
	9			8			7	
		5	1			6		
9					6	5		8
		3				7		
5		1	2					6
		4			7	1		
	7			5			4	
	3				4			

Puzzle 240

3				7	6	4		
	6	1	5					
	7		3	4				
1	9							
	2		7		4		6	
							2	3
				2	3		9	
					7	8	3	
		9	4	1				2

241

9		7				6		
			5		4	7	8	
				7			3	1
6		9			5			
1				3				4
			1			5		6
8	9			5				
	7	1	6		3			
		6				4		7

242

	4	3	2			1		
2			7					
			9				3	
5		2					4	1
1	3						9	6
9	8					2		3
	6				7			
					9			8
		8			1	9	6	

2 4 3

			5				3	
4	1							8
		8			6	4		
		3	7				6	9
	4						7	
9	5				8	2		
		4	8			7		
3							8	4
	2				5			

2 4 4

			7		4			9
			3		2	4		
				2	6			7
1							2	6
		2		6		8		
5	6							3
2		1	4					
	3	9		8				
4			2		9			

		9	6					
	8		2					
6	2	3	4	7			8	
						2	5	8
	1						9	
7	6	2						
	5			4	2	8	7	1
					7		3	
					6	4		

			3	9			8	5
		8					6	
5			6				7	
6					9			
		1		7		6		
			4					1
	2				1			4
	3					8		
7	5			6	2			

		5				3		
6				3	8		4	9
9								
8			5		9	4		
	6						2	
		1	2		6			3
								4
5	9		3	2				7
		8				6		

		4				6	5	
	7			4				
			3		5		9	
1			7			9	8	
		3				7		
	8	7			2			1
	4		9		1			
				5			3	
	2	9				8		

249

		9	8				6	
						9		
2	5		6	1				7
		1		3		5	2	
6								9
	4	5		2		7		
4				9	7		3	2
		3						
	1				3	8		

250

9		1				3		
6			1	4				9
	5		2				7	
1							8	
			8	2	1			
	3							4
	1				2		9	
2				9	8			3
		4				5		7

						9		7
	4				7		8	5
	6			9		1		
1				4			5	
		9		5		4		
	2			1				8
		2		3			9	
3	8		9				4	
6		1						

	3				7			
4				8	1	7		
	7		9		2		5	
		4				1		
	5		7		9		3	
		7				2		
	1		6		4		7	
		6	1	5				9
			2				4	

253

	3	7					9	
1						7		
	6		7	9	4	1		
6					5			
	9			2			5	
			3					9
		6	1	4	9		3	
		1						7
	4					6	2	

254

2				1	3			
			7			8		
	7				5			3
		1		4		5		6
	2		6		1		9	
3		6		7		4		
9			5				1	
		5			7			
			2	3				5

255

2							6	
6	8			2				4
5			7	4		8		
					5			
	9	6				5	3	
			1					
		1		5	9			7
7				6			4	1
	3							5

256

1				8			3	
2						4		
		5	1		4			
4					5		8	
6				2				3
	8		3					6
			5			1	6	
		1						9
	9			3				1

2 5 7

				1				
5						2	7	
7	4			9	5			
	7	5	8					2
			5		4			
3					7	5	8	
			9	5			1	3
	9	1						6
				7				

2 5 8

		4			3	2	7	
			1				4	5
				8				1
							6	7
	4		9	1	7		8	
7	2							
1				3				
2	9				1			
	6	3	8			1		

Puzzle 259:

7						8	6	
8		2			3	1		
	5			1				7
	8		3	6				
		6				5		
			9	4			8	
1				5			7	
		3	1			2		8
	7	4						1

Puzzle 260:

						7	9	
	6		8			2		
	1				4			
	4			3	2	1	5	
	9						3	
	7	1	4	9			2	
			9				4	
		9			3		7	
	2	6						

3					4		9	
	7	1				5		
5				7	8			
	6		9				1	
	3	2				9	7	
	9				2		5	
			6	4				5
		7				1	2	
	1		7					9

8	6		3		7			1
						6		
2					5		3	
			4		9		6	
3	9						1	2
	4		7		2			
	2		1					3
		5						
7			2		3		5	4

263

		3	5			7	9	
			1				3	
		8	7			5		4
			8		1		5	6
				4				
3	6		9		5			
1		4			7	9		
	8				9			
	2	7			6	8		

264

			5		4			
	2	4	9			1		8
	1							4
	8				5	3		
				9				
		2	8				9	
5							2	
3		1			7	9	6	
			4		1			

4		6	1					
3		7						5
		2		6			8	
	4				2			
		9		7		8		
			8				7	
	2			9		6		
6						3		9
					3	1		8

	4		5		3	9	8	
		2			8			
5						6	4	
				7	2			
8			3					7
		6	9					
	5	8						9
			6			8		
	6	4	8		9		7	

Puzzle 267:

5	3			4				
		7						1
			5		8	7		
8	7					2		
	1	2				4	6	
		4					7	9
		1	8		2			
4						1		
				6			2	7

Puzzle 268:

7				6		5		
9		3			1			7
							6	8
		1		3			4	2
6	2			4		1		
2	5							
4			7			9		6
		6		8				3

Puzzle 269:

	6			3				
4		9	5	8				2
		8	2					
3	8							
2			7		8			4
							8	5
				5	6			
1			2	9	7			8
			4			3		

Puzzle 270:

	8				1			
	1				5			2
			2	3	8			
8	3					4		
5	9			7			8	3
		4					2	9
		3	1	8				
6			2				4	
			4				6	

2
7
1

				7			9	
8		3	2			6		
					6	2		8
7						8		6
5				4				9
4		8						7
3		9	7					
		2			9	7		1
	7			3				

2
7
2

		6		9	4			
			6	3			1	
8			1				6	
6		1				4	7	
4								3
	9	7				8		1
	4				9			5
	5			4	1			
			5	7		2		

		9			4			
7		8			2			
4				3				9
5		3			8			
	6		4		7		3	
			6			4		1
9				8				7
			5			1		3
			7			6		

	7				9			4
	6				1			7
		4				9		6
4	8	5			2	7		
				1				
		1	5			2	4	8
2		7				4		
8			1				5	
3			8				7	

		4	7				2	
9				2	8			
				9	1		6	
	4					9		5
6	1						4	3
3		5					1	
	9		2	8				
			6	4				2
	2				7	3		

			7	1	8			
				3		2	6	
						7		1
		1	4			8	7	
7		4				9		5
	8	2			7	3		
5		9						
	1	8		4				
			1	7	2			

277

	1	4					7	
				8			6	
8	6		7	4		1	2	
		9				3		6
			2		6			
6		1				8		
	5	7		6	4		8	1
	4			1				
	8					6	5	

278

					8			
		3	9	4	1			
8	4	1		3				
1			7				4	
7				5				1
	3				9			8
				7		2	6	9
			4	9	2	3		
			8					

	2	8	1		9		4	
4			6		5			
		9				5		
						4		5
6			2		3			9
1		4						
		5				3		
			3		1			8
	8		5		4	6	1	

	7		8		6			
		1		7	4			
6								5
				1		5	3	8
	8						9	
2	1	3		8				
9								2
			4	6		8		
			9		8		5	

Puzzle 281

		8	4	9				2
	7				3			
2		3			5		8	
		6				2	1	9
3	4	1				6		
	9		6			8		3
			8				7	
8				3	2	5		

Puzzle 282

	7				6			
3			7	8	9			
	1	2						6
	4	9						7
			9		5			
1						5	4	
7						6	5	
			8	6	2			3
			4				9	

5			3	1			2	7
							6	
			9		2		8	
	3	4				8		
			2	9	8			
		2				1	5	
	7		6		3			
	4							
6	2			8	7			3

	3		2				9	
			5		3			4
7		2						3
8				5	6			
1	2						3	5
			1	2				9
3						9		8
2			6			1		
	8				5		6	

9					6	4	8	
		1			2	6	3	
6	2						7	
	7		5		1		6	
	9						5	4
	8	9	2			3		
	3	7	8					5

8	2						5	
	6					7		3
	7			9	1			
			2		7	5		
		1		5		4		
		2	1		4			
			3	1			7	
9		7					8	
	3						4	5

Puzzle 287

8			4			6		
		2			3		5	4
	7				9			
2	1					9		
	3			9			7	
		4					2	5
			5				6	
5	2		3			8		
		1			8			2

Puzzle 288

5		4			3			
					1			
			6	9			5	7
9			4			1		3
	4	5				8	2	
3		1			9			5
7	8			4	2			
			7					
			3			7		4

7	6							
	9	5		6		2	7	
								8
6			3	1			5	
	8	7		2		4	3	
	3			7	5			6
9								
	5	2		3		9	4	
							6	2

2	7						4	
			1	8				
4			7					3
	5				7	9		
	8			4			1	
		6	9				5	
5					9			1
				3	5			
	2						8	6

Puzzle 291:

	7		5		9			
1		6					9	
		9			1			
2					5		3	
	8		7		2		4	
	4		6					9
			1			6		
	2					9		8
			2		4		7	

Puzzle 292:

					7		6	
	8	6	2		1		5	
		2				1		3
		3					4	
	7		6		5		8	
	5				9			
2		1				7		
	3		7		6	8	1	
	6		1					

9			4					2
2					8			5
		8				1		4
		3	9			4		
	5		8		4		2	
		9			7	8		
8		4				5		
3			1					6
7					6			8

9		4	7					
	6			4				
7			5				3	
5		6		7		8		
			6		8			
		3		9		2		7
	3				2			6
				8			4	
					6	1		9

295

	7				1		6	
		1			3			
3						9		1
		6		5	2			
	3	5		1		2	7	
			3	4		5		
6		7						9
			6			3		
	1		7				2	

296

		2			8			
	4			7			9	
6		1	2		4			
1	6							8
		7	4			3	1	
2							7	6
			6		9	5		7
	8			1			4	
			7			6		

			4	3		1		
				8	1			4
	4	1				3		7
	9					5		
3			9		6			8
		8					2	
2		7				6	9	
1			5	2				
		9		6	7			

		5	3					8
				1	8			
8				9				7
	2	3					8	
5			7		1			6
	9					3	4	
3				5				4
			1	8				
7					9	6		

						9		2
						1	7	
4			5	7	2			
	2			8		3		
	8			1			2	
		7		6			9	
			7	2	6			1
	5	6						
8		1						

					4	9		
				2			6	
		2	9		3		7	
6	2	7						3
	5		7		2		9	
8						5	2	7
	8		1		6	4		
	9			5				
		6	4					

1

9	6	2	5	1	3	7	8	4
1	3	5	8	4	7	6	9	2
4	8	7	6	9	2	5	1	3
5	9	8	4	2	1	3	6	7
2	7	4	3	8	6	9	5	1
3	1	6	7	5	9	4	2	8
7	4	9	2	6	8	1	3	5
6	2	3	1	7	5	8	4	9
8	5	1	9	3	4	2	7	6

2

3	1	6	2	8	7	4	5	9
2	4	5	9	6	3	8	1	7
9	8	7	5	4	1	3	2	6
4	5	8	7	3	9	1	6	2
6	7	2	8	1	4	9	3	5
1	3	9	6	5	2	7	8	4
7	6	3	1	9	5	2	4	8
8	9	1	4	2	6	5	7	3
5	2	4	3	7	8	6	9	1

3

9	3	2	4	7	1	8	6	5
4	5	6	3	2	8	9	7	1
7	8	1	5	6	9	3	2	4
5	1	3	9	8	2	7	4	6
8	2	7	1	4	6	5	3	9
6	9	4	7	5	3	2	1	8
3	6	9	8	1	7	4	5	2
2	7	5	6	9	4	1	8	3
1	4	8	2	3	5	6	9	7

4

5	6	4	7	9	3	8	1	2
3	8	1	6	2	4	5	9	7
9	7	2	1	8	5	6	3	4
7	9	5	3	1	2	4	8	6
8	1	6	5	4	7	9	2	3
4	2	3	8	6	9	1	7	5
6	4	7	9	3	1	2	5	8
1	3	8	2	5	6	7	4	9
2	5	9	4	7	8	3	6	1

5

7	5	6	9	3	2	4	1	8
2	3	8	4	1	6	7	9	5
9	4	1	8	5	7	3	2	6
3	6	5	2	9	1	8	7	4
1	8	7	6	4	5	9	3	2
4	9	2	3	7	8	5	6	1
8	7	4	1	2	9	6	5	3
6	1	9	5	8	3	2	4	7
5	2	3	7	6	4	1	8	9

6

7	5	9	1	8	2	4	6	3
6	8	2	7	3	4	5	9	1
4	3	1	9	6	5	7	8	2
1	4	7	3	5	9	6	2	8
2	6	5	8	7	1	9	3	4
3	9	8	2	4	6	1	7	5
5	7	3	6	1	8	2	4	9
9	1	6	4	2	3	8	5	7
8	2	4	5	9	7	3	1	6

7

3	9	6	8	5	4	7	1	2
2	7	4	1	6	9	5	3	8
1	8	5	2	3	7	9	4	6
5	6	2	3	4	1	8	7	9
7	1	8	9	2	6	4	5	3
9	4	3	7	8	5	2	6	1
8	3	7	4	1	2	6	9	5
6	2	9	5	7	3	1	8	4
4	5	1	6	9	8	3	2	7

8

5	6	7	8	1	3	4	9	2
8	9	1	6	2	4	5	7	3
4	2	3	9	5	7	1	6	8
3	5	4	2	8	6	9	1	7
2	8	9	1	7	5	3	4	6
1	7	6	3	4	9	2	8	5
6	4	5	7	9	2	8	3	1
7	1	2	4	3	8	6	5	9
9	3	8	5	6	1	7	2	4

9

4	7	5	2	9	6	8	1	3
8	9	1	5	3	7	2	6	4
3	6	2	8	4	1	5	7	9
6	3	9	7	2	4	1	8	5
2	5	7	1	8	3	4	9	6
1	4	8	6	5	9	3	2	7
5	1	3	9	7	2	6	4	8
9	2	4	3	6	8	7	5	1
7	8	6	4	1	5	9	3	2

10

4	5	3	8	9	7	1	2	6
8	1	9	2	6	4	5	7	3
2	6	7	1	5	3	9	8	4
9	7	4	5	8	1	6	3	2
5	2	6	3	4	9	8	1	7
3	8	1	6	7	2	4	9	5
1	4	8	7	2	6	3	5	9
6	3	2	9	1	5	7	4	8
7	9	5	4	3	8	2	6	1

11

4	1	6	8	7	2	5	3	9
5	2	3	4	6	9	7	1	8
9	8	7	5	1	3	6	2	4
1	4	8	2	9	5	3	6	7
3	6	2	7	4	1	9	8	5
7	5	9	3	8	6	2	4	1
6	9	5	1	2	8	4	7	3
2	7	1	9	3	4	8	5	6
8	3	4	6	5	7	1	9	2

12

6	3	4	7	1	9	2	5	8
9	8	7	4	2	5	6	1	3
2	1	5	3	6	8	4	9	7
4	9	1	5	3	2	8	7	6
8	6	2	1	7	4	5	3	9
5	7	3	8	9	6	1	4	2
1	5	9	6	8	7	3	2	4
7	4	6	2	5	3	9	8	1
3	2	8	9	4	1	7	6	5

13

2	8	1	5	4	7	6	3	9
5	6	4	9	1	3	2	8	7
7	9	3	6	8	2	4	5	1
3	7	8	2	5	1	9	6	4
1	2	5	4	9	6	8	7	3
9	4	6	7	3	8	1	2	5
4	3	9	8	6	5	7	1	2
6	1	7	3	2	4	5	9	8
8	5	2	1	7	9	3	4	6

14

8	3	4	7	9	2	5	6	1
2	1	9	3	6	5	4	8	7
6	5	7	4	1	8	3	2	9
5	7	1	2	4	9	8	3	6
4	6	2	1	8	3	9	7	5
3	9	8	5	7	6	2	1	4
9	8	5	6	3	1	7	4	2
7	2	6	8	5	4	1	9	3
1	4	3	9	2	7	6	5	8

15

7	1	2	6	3	4	5	9	8
3	5	8	1	2	9	4	7	6
6	4	9	7	8	5	3	2	1
5	8	6	4	7	3	9	1	2
4	2	1	5	9	8	6	3	7
9	7	3	2	6	1	8	4	5
8	9	5	3	1	2	7	6	4
1	3	7	8	4	6	2	5	9
2	6	4	9	5	7	1	8	3

16

7	1	3	5	8	4	9	2	6
4	8	2	6	3	9	1	5	7
9	5	6	2	7	1	4	3	8
2	4	1	9	6	3	8	7	5
6	3	9	7	5	8	2	1	4
8	7	5	1	4	2	6	9	3
3	9	4	8	2	5	7	6	1
1	6	8	3	9	7	5	4	2
5	2	7	4	1	6	3	8	9

1 7

6	8	2	3	9	4	1	7	5
3	4	5	7	2	1	6	8	9
7	1	9	6	5	8	4	3	2
5	2	6	1	7	3	8	9	4
8	3	1	4	6	9	2	5	7
9	7	4	5	8	2	3	1	6
4	9	8	2	3	5	7	6	1
1	6	3	9	4	7	5	2	8
2	5	7	8	1	6	9	4	3

1 8

4	5	8	3	9	1	7	6	2
3	6	7	8	2	4	9	5	1
1	2	9	6	7	5	8	3	4
7	8	1	5	4	2	3	9	6
9	3	5	7	1	6	2	4	8
6	4	2	9	8	3	1	7	5
8	7	6	2	5	9	4	1	3
5	9	4	1	3	8	6	2	7
2	1	3	4	6	7	5	8	9

1 9

1	3	6	4	7	8	9	2	5
2	9	7	6	5	1	3	4	8
4	8	5	3	2	9	7	1	6
6	5	9	7	8	2	1	3	4
7	4	2	1	3	5	8	6	9
8	1	3	9	6	4	2	5	7
9	2	1	8	4	6	5	7	3
5	7	4	2	9	3	6	8	1
3	6	8	5	1	7	4	9	2

2 0

5	3	6	7	9	4	2	1	8
2	1	7	3	5	8	4	6	9
8	9	4	2	1	6	5	3	7
1	5	9	8	4	7	3	2	6
6	4	2	5	3	9	8	7	1
3	7	8	1	6	2	9	5	4
9	6	5	4	2	1	7	8	3
4	8	3	6	7	5	1	9	2
7	2	1	9	8	3	6	4	5

2 1

3	2	6	5	4	7	8	1	9
5	9	4	8	1	3	7	6	2
7	8	1	9	2	6	4	3	5
8	7	9	2	3	5	1	4	6
4	3	5	1	6	8	2	9	7
6	1	2	7	9	4	5	8	3
2	6	7	3	8	1	9	5	4
9	4	8	6	5	2	3	7	1
1	5	3	4	7	9	6	2	8

2 2

1	3	4	8	6	7	9	2	5
2	9	7	1	3	5	4	6	8
8	6	5	4	2	9	7	1	3
4	5	8	2	7	6	3	9	1
7	1	3	9	4	8	6	5	2
9	2	6	3	5	1	8	7	4
6	8	1	5	9	3	2	4	7
5	4	9	7	8	2	1	3	6
3	7	2	6	1	4	5	8	9

2 3

1	9	3	4	7	6	5	2	8
7	4	6	8	2	5	9	3	1
5	2	8	3	1	9	7	4	6
4	5	7	6	3	1	8	9	2
2	3	9	5	4	8	1	6	7
6	8	1	7	9	2	3	5	4
9	7	4	1	6	3	2	8	5
3	6	5	2	8	7	4	1	9
8	1	2	9	5	4	6	7	3

2 4

5	1	8	3	9	6	7	2	4
3	2	7	8	1	4	5	9	6
4	6	9	2	7	5	8	1	3
1	3	6	9	8	7	4	5	2
2	7	5	4	6	3	1	8	9
8	9	4	5	2	1	3	6	7
6	4	2	1	3	8	9	7	5
7	5	1	6	4	9	2	3	8
9	8	3	7	5	2	6	4	1

2/5

6	1	2	5	8	4	9	3	7
4	3	9	7	2	1	6	8	5
8	5	7	6	9	3	1	2	4
5	6	1	2	7	9	3	4	8
3	2	8	1	4	5	7	6	9
9	7	4	8	3	6	5	1	2
7	8	3	9	6	2	4	5	1
1	9	6	4	5	8	2	7	3
2	4	5	3	1	7	8	9	6

2/6

8	2	7	5	9	3	4	1	6
9	5	4	6	2	1	8	3	7
3	6	1	8	7	4	5	9	2
1	7	9	2	6	8	3	4	5
5	8	2	4	3	9	6	7	1
6	4	3	1	5	7	9	2	8
4	3	6	7	1	5	2	8	9
2	1	8	9	4	6	7	5	3
7	9	5	3	8	2	1	6	4

2/7

9	3	8	5	2	4	7	6	1
7	4	1	3	9	6	2	5	8
2	6	5	8	7	1	4	3	9
5	2	9	4	8	7	3	1	6
4	1	7	6	3	5	8	9	2
6	8	3	9	1	2	5	4	7
1	9	2	7	4	3	6	8	5
8	5	4	2	6	9	1	7	3
3	7	6	1	5	8	9	2	4

2/8

9	2	6	1	8	3	5	4	7
8	3	1	4	7	5	2	9	6
7	5	4	9	2	6	1	8	3
6	1	9	3	4	8	7	2	5
4	7	5	6	1	2	9	3	8
3	8	2	5	9	7	6	1	4
5	9	3	2	6	4	8	7	1
1	6	8	7	3	9	4	5	2
2	4	7	8	5	1	3	6	9

2/9

6	3	1	7	5	2	8	9	4
2	9	4	8	6	1	7	3	5
5	8	7	9	4	3	1	2	6
7	2	8	5	9	4	6	1	3
1	6	5	2	3	7	9	4	8
9	4	3	6	1	8	5	7	2
8	1	2	3	7	5	4	6	9
4	5	6	1	2	9	3	8	7
3	7	9	4	8	6	2	5	1

3/0

4	6	2	8	5	1	3	9	7
3	1	9	4	7	6	2	5	8
5	8	7	3	2	9	1	4	6
6	3	1	2	8	4	5	7	9
9	7	5	1	6	3	8	2	4
8	2	4	7	9	5	6	1	3
2	5	8	9	3	7	4	6	1
7	4	3	6	1	2	9	8	5
1	9	6	5	4	8	7	3	2

3/1

5	4	8	1	6	3	2	7	9
3	9	2	7	5	4	6	8	1
6	7	1	9	8	2	3	5	4
7	2	6	4	3	8	9	1	5
4	1	5	2	9	6	7	3	8
9	8	3	5	1	7	4	2	6
1	3	7	6	4	5	8	9	2
8	5	4	3	2	9	1	6	7
2	6	9	8	7	1	5	4	3

3/2

1	2	4	6	7	5	8	9	3
3	7	6	4	8	9	5	1	2
9	5	8	2	1	3	7	4	6
2	4	3	1	9	7	6	8	5
5	9	1	3	6	8	4	2	7
6	8	7	5	2	4	1	3	9
4	3	9	8	5	6	2	7	1
8	1	5	7	3	2	9	6	4
7	6	2	9	4	1	3	5	8

3 3

2	5	7	9	6	4	8	3	1
8	6	3	1	7	5	4	2	9
4	1	9	3	8	2	5	6	7
1	8	4	2	9	6	3	7	5
5	3	6	7	1	8	9	4	2
7	9	2	5	4	3	6	1	8
6	7	8	4	5	1	2	9	3
9	2	5	6	3	7	1	8	4
3	4	1	8	2	9	7	5	6

3 4

9	8	6	3	1	7	2	5	4
5	4	1	6	8	2	9	7	3
3	7	2	9	4	5	6	8	1
1	9	8	2	5	3	7	4	6
4	3	5	8	7	6	1	2	9
2	6	7	1	9	4	5	3	8
7	1	9	5	3	8	4	6	2
6	5	3	4	2	1	8	9	7
8	2	4	7	6	9	3	1	5

3 5

7	9	6	1	3	5	2	4	8
1	8	5	9	2	4	6	3	7
2	4	3	8	6	7	9	5	1
5	2	9	4	1	3	7	8	6
3	7	4	6	9	8	5	1	2
8	6	1	7	5	2	3	9	4
6	3	2	5	8	1	4	7	9
9	1	7	3	4	6	8	2	5
4	5	8	2	7	9	1	6	3

3 6

6	4	3	1	5	8	2	7	9
5	8	2	6	9	7	1	3	4
7	1	9	3	2	4	8	5	6
9	6	4	7	1	3	5	8	2
2	7	5	4	8	9	3	6	1
1	3	8	2	6	5	9	4	7
3	5	6	9	4	2	7	1	8
4	9	7	8	3	1	6	2	5
8	2	1	5	7	6	4	9	3

3 7

9	4	8	2	3	5	6	1	7
3	7	5	6	1	9	2	4	8
6	2	1	4	8	7	9	3	5
7	8	4	5	2	6	3	9	1
1	9	6	7	4	3	8	5	2
5	3	2	8	9	1	4	7	6
8	1	3	9	5	2	7	6	4
4	6	9	1	7	8	5	2	3
2	5	7	3	6	4	1	8	9

3 8

8	5	1	7	3	2	6	9	4
7	3	6	1	9	4	8	5	2
4	2	9	8	6	5	3	7	1
2	4	5	9	8	7	1	3	6
9	7	3	6	4	1	5	2	8
1	6	8	5	2	3	7	4	9
3	9	7	4	1	8	2	6	5
6	8	2	3	5	9	4	1	7
5	1	4	2	7	6	9	8	3

3 9

6	1	4	2	3	8	5	9	7
7	5	8	6	4	9	1	2	3
3	2	9	5	1	7	8	4	6
9	4	2	7	8	1	6	3	5
8	6	1	9	5	3	4	7	2
5	3	7	4	2	6	9	8	1
1	9	3	8	6	2	7	5	4
4	7	6	3	9	5	2	1	8
2	8	5	1	7	4	3	6	9

4 0

8	1	3	9	4	2	5	6	7
7	5	4	3	1	6	9	8	2
9	6	2	7	8	5	3	1	4
4	9	7	2	6	3	1	5	8
5	3	1	8	7	4	2	9	6
2	8	6	5	9	1	4	7	3
6	4	8	1	2	9	7	3	5
3	2	9	6	5	7	8	4	1
1	7	5	4	3	8	6	2	9

4/1

8	6	5	7	3	9	2	4	1
1	3	2	8	4	6	9	5	7
4	9	7	2	5	1	3	8	6
6	1	4	5	2	3	7	9	8
7	8	9	6	1	4	5	2	3
5	2	3	9	7	8	6	1	4
9	7	1	3	8	5	4	6	2
3	5	8	4	6	2	1	7	9
2	4	6	1	9	7	8	3	5

4/2

9	3	6	2	5	7	4	1	8
5	2	7	4	8	1	6	3	9
4	1	8	9	6	3	7	5	2
7	4	2	8	1	5	3	9	6
8	5	9	3	4	6	1	2	7
1	6	3	7	9	2	5	8	4
2	8	1	6	3	4	9	7	5
3	9	4	5	7	8	2	6	1
6	7	5	1	2	9	8	4	3

4/3

3	2	8	5	4	9	1	6	7
1	5	6	7	2	3	8	9	4
9	7	4	6	8	1	5	2	3
7	6	1	8	3	5	2	4	9
5	8	9	4	6	2	7	3	1
4	3	2	9	1	7	6	8	5
6	4	7	3	5	8	9	1	2
2	9	3	1	7	6	4	5	8
8	1	5	2	9	4	3	7	6

4/4

8	3	6	4	5	1	2	7	9
7	1	4	8	2	9	5	3	6
2	9	5	7	6	3	8	4	1
5	8	9	3	1	4	7	6	2
1	2	3	5	7	6	4	9	8
4	6	7	2	9	8	1	5	3
9	4	2	6	8	5	3	1	7
6	5	8	1	3	7	9	2	4
3	7	1	9	4	2	6	8	5

4/5

1	7	6	5	8	3	2	9	4
5	9	8	6	2	4	1	3	7
2	3	4	1	9	7	6	8	5
3	4	2	8	6	9	5	7	1
8	1	9	4	7	5	3	2	6
7	6	5	2	3	1	8	4	9
4	8	7	3	5	6	9	1	2
9	5	3	7	1	2	4	6	8
6	2	1	9	4	8	7	5	3

4/6

2	6	9	8	5	4	7	3	1
8	1	3	7	2	6	5	4	9
7	5	4	9	1	3	2	8	6
5	3	8	6	9	7	4	1	2
6	2	1	5	4	8	3	9	7
9	4	7	2	3	1	6	5	8
1	8	6	4	7	5	9	2	3
4	7	2	3	8	9	1	6	5
3	9	5	1	6	2	8	7	4

4/7

1	2	9	7	3	6	5	8	4
6	4	7	9	5	8	1	2	3
8	5	3	2	4	1	6	7	9
9	3	8	6	1	7	4	5	2
4	7	1	3	2	5	9	6	8
2	6	5	4	8	9	7	3	1
7	8	2	5	9	4	3	1	6
3	9	6	1	7	2	8	4	5
5	1	4	8	6	3	2	9	7

4/8

9	6	8	2	3	5	1	4	7
2	5	3	1	4	7	8	6	9
7	4	1	8	6	9	5	3	2
3	1	2	9	5	6	7	8	4
6	9	7	4	1	8	2	5	3
4	8	5	7	2	3	6	9	1
5	7	6	3	9	2	4	1	8
1	2	9	5	8	4	3	7	6
8	3	4	6	7	1	9	2	5

49

1	9	3	5	7	4	2	6	8
2	8	4	1	6	3	5	9	7
7	6	5	2	8	9	1	4	3
3	1	9	6	2	8	4	7	5
4	7	8	3	1	5	6	2	9
6	5	2	4	9	7	8	3	1
9	2	7	8	4	1	3	5	6
8	3	6	7	5	2	9	1	4
5	4	1	9	3	6	7	8	2

50

4	8	1	2	9	7	3	6	5
3	7	9	6	5	8	1	4	2
2	5	6	4	1	3	7	8	9
7	6	4	5	2	1	9	3	8
5	9	2	8	3	4	6	1	7
8	1	3	7	6	9	2	5	4
6	2	8	3	7	5	4	9	1
9	4	7	1	8	6	5	2	3
1	3	5	9	4	2	8	7	6

51

6	5	7	8	3	1	2	9	4
1	2	9	5	7	4	8	3	6
3	8	4	6	9	2	7	5	1
8	6	1	7	2	5	3	4	9
5	7	2	9	4	3	6	1	8
4	9	3	1	8	6	5	7	2
9	3	5	4	6	8	1	2	7
2	4	8	3	1	7	9	6	5
7	1	6	2	5	9	4	8	3

52

5	1	7	2	6	9	3	4	8
3	8	4	7	1	5	2	9	6
9	2	6	3	8	4	5	1	7
7	9	3	1	2	8	6	5	4
8	5	1	6	4	7	9	3	2
6	4	2	5	9	3	7	8	1
4	6	8	9	3	2	1	7	5
2	7	9	8	5	1	4	6	3
1	3	5	4	7	6	8	2	9

53

5	9	7	8	3	1	2	6	4
4	6	3	2	7	5	9	8	1
2	1	8	9	6	4	5	3	7
8	4	2	1	9	3	6	7	5
6	5	9	7	8	2	1	4	3
7	3	1	5	4	6	8	2	9
3	7	5	6	1	8	4	9	2
1	8	4	3	2	9	7	5	6
9	2	6	4	5	7	3	1	8

54

7	2	8	4	5	6	3	1	9
9	3	6	2	8	1	4	5	7
5	1	4	3	7	9	8	2	6
6	4	9	5	2	8	7	3	1
3	5	1	7	6	4	9	8	2
2	8	7	1	9	3	5	6	4
1	9	5	8	4	2	6	7	3
4	7	3	6	1	5	2	9	8
8	6	2	9	3	7	1	4	5

55

8	9	1	3	4	2	6	7	5
5	2	4	7	9	6	3	1	8
6	3	7	5	8	1	2	9	4
1	4	3	8	5	7	9	2	6
7	6	2	9	1	4	5	8	3
9	8	5	6	2	3	1	4	7
2	7	8	1	3	5	4	6	9
3	1	6	4	7	9	8	5	2
4	5	9	2	6	8	7	3	1

56

7	9	8	2	1	6	5	4	3
3	1	4	5	7	9	8	6	2
6	2	5	4	8	3	7	1	9
2	4	7	9	5	8	6	3	1
9	8	6	1	3	4	2	7	5
1	5	3	6	2	7	4	9	8
8	6	2	3	4	1	9	5	7
4	7	1	8	9	5	3	2	6
5	3	9	7	6	2	1	8	4

57

5	7	3	6	4	9	8	1	2
9	1	4	2	8	7	5	6	3
2	6	8	5	1	3	7	9	4
4	3	1	9	2	8	6	7	5
8	9	2	7	5	6	3	4	1
7	5	6	1	3	4	2	8	9
1	2	7	8	9	5	4	3	6
6	4	9	3	7	2	1	5	8
3	8	5	4	6	1	9	2	7

58

5	6	7	3	8	1	4	2	9
4	9	3	5	6	2	8	7	1
2	1	8	4	7	9	3	6	5
8	7	6	1	2	3	9	5	4
1	5	4	8	9	6	2	3	7
3	2	9	7	4	5	1	8	6
9	8	2	6	1	7	5	4	3
7	3	1	2	5	4	6	9	8
6	4	5	9	3	8	7	1	2

59

9	3	6	4	5	1	8	7	2
7	5	1	9	2	8	3	6	4
2	4	8	3	7	6	1	5	9
8	2	9	6	1	4	7	3	5
4	7	3	5	8	2	9	1	6
6	1	5	7	3	9	4	2	8
5	8	4	1	6	7	2	9	3
3	9	7	2	4	5	6	8	1
1	6	2	8	9	3	5	4	7

60

4	5	7	8	9	3	2	1	6
2	3	1	5	4	6	9	8	7
6	8	9	2	1	7	5	3	4
1	7	2	4	5	9	8	6	3
8	6	5	1	3	2	4	7	9
9	4	3	6	7	8	1	5	2
3	1	4	7	2	5	6	9	8
5	9	6	3	8	4	7	2	1
7	2	8	9	6	1	3	4	5

61

9	6	2	5	1	8	4	3	7
1	7	4	9	3	2	6	5	8
8	5	3	6	4	7	1	2	9
4	3	1	8	7	6	2	9	5
7	8	5	2	9	4	3	6	1
6	2	9	1	5	3	7	8	4
2	9	7	3	8	1	5	4	6
5	4	6	7	2	9	8	1	3
3	1	8	4	6	5	9	7	2

62

1	8	4	3	5	6	9	7	2
3	5	2	1	7	9	8	6	4
6	7	9	2	4	8	3	1	5
2	1	3	6	8	5	7	4	9
7	9	5	4	2	1	6	3	8
8	4	6	7	9	3	5	2	1
4	6	8	9	3	2	1	5	7
5	3	7	8	1	4	2	9	6
9	2	1	5	6	7	4	8	3

63

5	9	4	3	6	7	2	8	1
7	8	3	2	9	1	4	5	6
6	2	1	5	8	4	3	7	9
3	4	5	1	2	9	8	6	7
9	1	2	6	7	8	5	4	3
8	7	6	4	3	5	1	9	2
1	5	7	9	4	2	6	3	8
4	6	9	8	1	3	7	2	5
2	3	8	7	5	6	9	1	4

64

1	5	8	4	7	3	6	2	9
9	2	7	5	6	1	3	8	4
6	4	3	2	8	9	7	5	1
4	9	6	1	2	5	8	3	7
3	7	2	9	4	8	1	6	5
8	1	5	7	3	6	9	4	2
2	3	1	6	9	4	5	7	8
7	6	9	8	5	2	4	1	3
5	8	4	3	1	7	2	9	6

65

3	8	2	9	7	6	4	1	5
7	9	5	3	4	1	2	6	8
6	4	1	8	2	5	9	3	7
4	6	9	2	5	3	8	7	1
2	5	7	6	1	8	3	9	4
1	3	8	4	9	7	6	5	2
9	1	4	7	6	2	5	8	3
8	7	6	5	3	4	1	2	9
5	2	3	1	8	9	7	4	6

66

8	9	6	7	2	5	4	1	3
1	7	3	8	9	4	5	6	2
4	5	2	3	1	6	9	8	7
9	8	5	6	7	1	2	3	4
7	3	1	4	8	2	6	9	5
2	6	4	5	3	9	8	7	1
5	2	7	1	6	8	3	4	9
6	1	9	2	4	3	7	5	8
3	4	8	9	5	7	1	2	6

67

2	3	8	7	6	5	4	1	9
6	7	5	1	4	9	3	2	8
4	1	9	2	8	3	7	5	6
7	9	4	5	1	2	8	6	3
1	2	6	9	3	8	5	7	4
8	5	3	6	7	4	2	9	1
5	8	7	4	9	1	6	3	2
9	4	2	3	5	6	1	8	7
3	6	1	8	2	7	9	4	5

68

9	2	7	1	3	5	4	6	8
5	4	1	8	2	6	7	3	9
8	3	6	4	9	7	1	2	5
4	5	8	3	7	2	9	1	6
2	1	3	6	8	9	5	4	7
6	7	9	5	1	4	2	8	3
3	9	2	7	4	8	6	5	1
1	6	4	9	5	3	8	7	2
7	8	5	2	6	1	3	9	4

69

9	1	8	7	6	3	5	2	4
7	6	5	8	4	2	3	1	9
2	4	3	5	1	9	6	7	8
8	9	2	6	7	4	1	5	3
4	5	6	3	9	1	7	8	2
3	7	1	2	5	8	9	4	6
5	3	7	4	2	6	8	9	1
1	8	4	9	3	7	2	6	5
6	2	9	1	8	5	4	3	7

70

1	9	4	2	3	8	5	6	7
6	2	7	4	1	5	9	8	3
8	5	3	7	6	9	4	2	1
7	6	9	8	5	1	2	3	4
2	3	5	6	7	4	1	9	8
4	8	1	3	9	2	6	7	5
5	7	2	1	8	6	3	4	9
9	4	8	5	2	3	7	1	6
3	1	6	9	4	7	8	5	2

71

7	2	9	1	6	4	5	3	8
3	8	1	9	7	5	2	6	4
4	5	6	8	2	3	1	7	9
1	9	8	3	5	7	4	2	6
2	4	7	6	8	9	3	5	1
5	6	3	4	1	2	9	8	7
8	1	5	2	4	6	7	9	3
9	7	4	5	3	8	6	1	2
6	3	2	7	9	1	8	4	5

72

5	9	4	2	6	3	8	1	7
7	8	6	9	1	5	3	4	2
3	1	2	4	8	7	6	9	5
8	6	5	7	3	4	1	2	9
9	7	1	6	2	8	4	5	3
4	2	3	1	5	9	7	6	8
6	5	8	3	9	1	2	7	4
2	4	9	8	7	6	5	3	1
1	3	7	5	4	2	9	8	6

7/3

9	2	4	7	6	1	3	8	5
5	7	6	9	3	8	2	1	4
3	8	1	5	2	4	7	6	9
8	3	7	6	4	2	5	9	1
1	5	9	3	8	7	6	4	2
4	6	2	1	5	9	8	3	7
7	4	8	2	9	3	1	5	6
6	1	3	4	7	5	9	2	8
2	9	5	8	1	6	4	7	3

7/4

2	1	5	9	4	8	7	6	3
4	7	3	2	5	6	9	1	8
9	8	6	3	1	7	5	4	2
3	5	4	8	6	1	2	9	7
8	2	7	4	9	5	6	3	1
1	6	9	7	3	2	8	5	4
6	4	2	1	7	9	3	8	5
7	9	1	5	8	3	4	2	6
5	3	8	6	2	4	1	7	9

7/5

2	4	7	1	3	6	8	5	9
8	5	9	4	2	7	6	1	3
3	6	1	9	8	5	2	7	4
1	3	4	6	7	9	5	8	2
7	9	8	2	5	3	4	6	1
6	2	5	8	4	1	3	9	7
5	7	6	3	9	4	1	2	8
9	8	3	5	1	2	7	4	6
4	1	2	7	6	8	9	3	5

7/6

6	7	8	5	4	2	9	1	3
4	9	1	7	6	3	5	8	2
5	2	3	9	8	1	6	7	4
7	4	9	6	2	8	1	3	5
3	8	6	1	5	9	2	4	7
2	1	5	3	7	4	8	6	9
9	6	2	8	3	7	4	5	1
1	5	7	4	9	6	3	2	8
8	3	4	2	1	5	7	9	6

7/7

4	8	3	6	2	1	9	5	7
5	2	1	3	7	9	6	8	4
6	9	7	5	8	4	1	2	3
7	6	5	2	4	3	8	9	1
2	4	8	9	1	7	3	6	5
1	3	9	8	6	5	4	7	2
3	7	2	4	9	8	5	1	6
8	5	6	1	3	2	7	4	9
9	1	4	7	5	6	2	3	8

7/8

8	6	3	2	9	1	4	5	7
5	9	7	4	8	3	1	2	6
4	2	1	7	5	6	9	8	3
2	8	9	3	6	7	5	4	1
6	7	4	9	1	5	2	3	8
1	3	5	8	2	4	6	7	9
9	1	8	5	3	2	7	6	4
3	4	2	6	7	9	8	1	5
7	5	6	1	4	8	3	9	2

7/9

3	2	1	8	6	7	5	4	9
4	5	7	3	2	9	8	1	6
6	8	9	4	1	5	3	2	7
5	1	6	2	3	4	7	9	8
7	3	8	6	9	1	4	5	2
2	9	4	7	5	8	6	3	1
8	4	3	9	7	2	1	6	5
9	6	5	1	8	3	2	7	4
1	7	2	5	4	6	9	8	3

8/0

6	1	3	7	4	8	5	2	9
9	8	4	6	2	5	3	1	7
2	7	5	9	3	1	6	8	4
1	5	6	2	9	3	4	7	8
8	3	9	1	7	4	2	6	5
4	2	7	5	8	6	9	3	1
3	6	8	4	5	7	1	9	2
5	9	1	8	6	2	7	4	3
7	4	2	3	1	9	8	5	6

8-1

6	3	7	2	5	9	1	4	8
1	5	8	4	7	3	2	6	9
9	4	2	8	6	1	5	3	7
5	6	9	7	2	4	3	8	1
2	1	4	5	3	8	7	9	6
8	7	3	9	1	6	4	5	2
4	2	1	6	9	5	8	7	3
3	9	5	1	8	7	6	2	4
7	8	6	3	4	2	9	1	5

8-2

1	9	2	8	4	5	3	7	6
3	6	4	9	7	1	5	2	8
8	7	5	3	2	6	4	9	1
9	1	6	7	5	2	8	4	3
5	8	3	4	6	9	7	1	2
4	2	7	1	8	3	9	6	5
7	5	8	2	1	4	6	3	9
6	3	1	5	9	7	2	8	4
2	4	9	6	3	8	1	5	7

8-3

8	1	5	2	3	4	7	6	9
3	9	7	1	8	6	4	2	5
4	2	6	7	9	5	3	1	8
2	6	1	5	4	3	9	8	7
7	4	3	8	2	9	6	5	1
5	8	9	6	7	1	2	4	3
1	5	4	3	6	7	8	9	2
9	7	8	4	1	2	5	3	6
6	3	2	9	5	8	1	7	4

8-4

4	3	9	8	7	2	1	6	5
1	5	6	3	4	9	2	8	7
2	7	8	6	1	5	9	3	4
3	4	5	9	6	8	7	1	2
9	2	7	1	5	3	8	4	6
6	8	1	4	2	7	5	9	3
5	1	4	7	9	6	3	2	8
7	6	3	2	8	1	4	5	9
8	9	2	5	3	4	6	7	1

8-5

2	6	7	4	5	1	3	8	9
5	8	1	6	9	3	2	7	4
3	9	4	7	8	2	6	5	1
8	1	3	5	4	9	7	2	6
4	2	6	3	7	8	9	1	5
7	5	9	1	2	6	4	3	8
1	4	2	9	3	5	8	6	7
6	7	8	2	1	4	5	9	3
9	3	5	8	6	7	1	4	2

8-6

9	6	3	7	1	8	2	4	5
7	5	4	6	2	9	3	1	8
1	2	8	4	5	3	9	6	7
8	4	7	3	6	1	5	2	9
3	9	6	2	8	5	4	7	1
5	1	2	9	4	7	8	3	6
2	3	1	8	9	6	7	5	4
4	8	5	1	7	2	6	9	3
6	7	9	5	3	4	1	8	2

8-7

2	4	8	5	6	1	7	9	3
7	3	5	2	8	9	4	6	1
9	6	1	7	3	4	5	8	2
6	9	2	4	1	7	8	3	5
1	7	4	8	5	3	9	2	6
5	8	3	9	2	6	1	4	7
4	1	6	3	9	5	2	7	8
8	5	7	6	4	2	3	1	9
3	2	9	1	7	8	6	5	4

8-8

5	8	9	4	2	3	1	7	6
4	2	3	1	6	7	9	5	8
7	1	6	5	8	9	3	4	2
2	4	8	7	5	1	6	3	9
3	7	1	2	9	6	5	8	4
9	6	5	3	4	8	2	1	7
8	5	4	6	1	2	7	9	3
6	9	7	8	3	5	4	2	1
1	3	2	9	7	4	8	6	5

8/9

8	2	1	5	9	6	3	7	4
5	6	4	3	1	7	9	2	8
3	9	7	4	8	2	1	6	5
6	8	5	7	2	3	4	9	1
9	4	2	8	6	1	7	5	3
1	7	3	9	5	4	2	8	6
2	5	8	1	3	9	6	4	7
4	1	9	6	7	8	5	3	2
7	3	6	2	4	5	8	1	9

9/0

2	8	7	9	5	1	4	3	6
9	6	4	3	2	8	5	1	7
1	3	5	7	6	4	2	8	9
8	4	3	6	9	2	7	5	1
5	2	9	4	1	7	3	6	8
6	7	1	8	3	5	9	2	4
4	5	2	1	8	9	6	7	3
7	1	6	2	4	3	8	9	5
3	9	8	5	7	6	1	4	2

9/1

7	6	1	9	8	3	5	2	4
9	5	3	1	4	2	6	8	7
4	2	8	5	7	6	1	9	3
8	7	5	6	3	1	9	4	2
6	9	2	4	5	8	3	7	1
1	3	4	2	9	7	8	5	6
5	1	9	7	6	4	2	3	8
3	4	6	8	2	5	7	1	9
2	8	7	3	1	9	4	6	5

9/2

3	5	9	4	8	2	7	1	6
4	8	2	1	6	7	5	9	3
6	7	1	5	3	9	4	2	8
5	6	7	2	9	3	8	4	1
8	1	4	7	5	6	2	3	9
2	9	3	8	1	4	6	5	7
7	3	5	9	4	8	1	6	2
1	2	6	3	7	5	9	8	4
9	4	8	6	2	1	3	7	5

9/3

6	3	1	8	4	5	7	9	2
5	4	7	1	9	2	8	6	3
9	8	2	3	7	6	4	5	1
7	2	6	9	8	1	5	3	4
4	9	5	6	2	3	1	8	7
8	1	3	4	5	7	9	2	6
1	7	9	2	6	8	3	4	5
3	6	4	5	1	9	2	7	8
2	5	8	7	3	4	6	1	9

9/4

6	4	2	9	8	7	1	3	5
1	8	7	6	5	3	9	4	2
9	3	5	2	1	4	6	7	8
5	9	4	3	6	1	8	2	7
3	1	8	5	7	2	4	9	6
2	7	6	4	9	8	3	5	1
8	6	9	7	4	5	2	1	3
7	2	1	8	3	9	5	6	4
4	5	3	1	2	6	7	8	9

9/5

3	9	6	5	8	4	7	1	2
4	7	2	9	3	1	8	5	6
8	1	5	6	2	7	9	3	4
7	4	1	8	5	9	2	6	3
9	2	8	4	6	3	5	7	1
5	6	3	7	1	2	4	8	9
6	5	9	3	4	8	1	2	7
2	8	4	1	7	6	3	9	5
1	3	7	2	9	5	6	4	8

9/6

3	6	9	4	1	8	2	5	7
7	1	4	9	5	2	6	3	8
8	5	2	7	3	6	1	9	4
2	9	7	5	4	1	8	6	3
5	3	1	8	6	7	9	4	2
4	8	6	3	2	9	7	1	5
1	7	5	6	8	3	4	2	9
6	4	8	2	9	5	3	7	1
9	2	3	1	7	4	5	8	6

97

6	8	7	1	4	3	9	5	2
2	4	9	7	6	5	3	1	8
1	5	3	2	9	8	4	7	6
9	3	2	8	5	7	6	4	1
8	1	5	4	2	6	7	3	9
7	6	4	3	1	9	8	2	5
4	7	6	5	8	1	2	9	3
3	9	1	6	7	2	5	8	4
5	2	8	9	3	4	1	6	7

98

2	5	4	3	8	7	1	9	6
6	7	8	5	9	1	3	2	4
3	1	9	4	2	6	5	7	8
4	3	5	7	6	2	8	1	9
7	2	1	8	5	9	6	4	3
9	8	6	1	3	4	2	5	7
5	6	2	9	4	8	7	3	1
8	9	7	2	1	3	4	6	5
1	4	3	6	7	5	9	8	2

99

1	9	6	7	8	5	3	4	2
2	4	3	6	1	9	8	5	7
5	8	7	3	2	4	6	9	1
4	5	9	2	3	7	1	6	8
3	7	1	9	6	8	4	2	5
6	2	8	5	4	1	7	3	9
9	3	5	8	7	6	2	1	4
8	1	2	4	5	3	9	7	6
7	6	4	1	9	2	5	8	3

100

8	6	1	9	5	2	7	4	3
4	5	2	1	3	7	6	9	8
7	9	3	6	4	8	5	2	1
9	8	5	7	6	3	2	1	4
1	7	4	8	2	9	3	6	5
2	3	6	4	1	5	9	8	7
5	2	8	3	9	4	1	7	6
3	1	7	2	8	6	4	5	9
6	4	9	5	7	1	8	3	2

101

3	7	8	4	5	1	6	9	2
2	1	9	8	3	6	5	4	7
5	6	4	9	7	2	1	8	3
4	9	2	6	8	3	7	5	1
8	3	7	1	4	5	2	6	9
1	5	6	2	9	7	8	3	4
9	4	1	5	2	8	3	7	6
7	2	5	3	6	9	4	1	8
6	8	3	7	1	4	9	2	5

102

6	3	4	8	2	7	9	1	5
9	8	7	3	1	5	2	6	4
2	5	1	6	4	9	8	7	3
7	6	8	9	3	4	1	5	2
4	9	3	1	5	2	6	8	7
1	2	5	7	8	6	4	3	9
8	4	2	5	6	3	7	9	1
3	1	9	4	7	8	5	2	6
5	7	6	2	9	1	3	4	8

103

8	1	3	5	6	2	4	7	9
4	7	5	9	1	8	6	2	3
2	9	6	3	7	4	5	1	8
3	4	9	1	5	6	7	8	2
7	2	1	4	8	3	9	5	6
5	6	8	7	2	9	3	4	1
1	5	2	6	3	7	8	9	4
6	8	4	2	9	5	1	3	7
9	3	7	8	4	1	2	6	5

104

9	8	4	2	5	6	7	3	1
7	2	5	4	3	1	9	8	6
1	3	6	9	8	7	5	2	4
8	9	1	5	6	4	3	7	2
2	6	3	8	7	9	1	4	5
5	4	7	3	1	2	6	9	8
3	5	2	6	9	8	4	1	7
4	1	9	7	2	5	8	6	3
6	7	8	1	4	3	2	5	9

105

1	3	5	7	2	8	9	6	4
6	2	9	4	1	3	7	5	8
7	4	8	5	6	9	3	2	1
2	8	7	1	9	4	5	3	6
9	5	6	3	8	7	1	4	2
4	1	3	2	5	6	8	9	7
3	6	1	9	7	2	4	8	5
5	9	2	8	4	1	6	7	3
8	7	4	6	3	5	2	1	9

106

7	3	8	9	5	4	1	6	2
1	9	5	7	2	6	3	4	8
4	6	2	3	1	8	9	5	7
5	4	6	8	7	3	2	1	9
2	7	3	5	9	1	6	8	4
9	8	1	4	6	2	5	7	3
6	1	7	2	4	9	8	3	5
3	5	9	1	8	7	4	2	6
8	2	4	6	3	5	7	9	1

107

8	1	4	3	5	9	7	2	6
3	7	6	1	2	8	9	5	4
5	9	2	6	4	7	3	1	8
4	3	1	7	6	5	8	9	2
7	6	8	4	9	2	1	3	5
2	5	9	8	1	3	6	4	7
1	4	3	2	7	6	5	8	9
6	2	5	9	8	1	4	7	3
9	8	7	5	3	4	2	6	1

108

4	8	5	6	3	2	9	1	7
1	7	2	5	4	9	8	3	6
6	9	3	1	7	8	2	4	5
8	5	7	3	9	1	4	6	2
2	1	6	8	5	4	7	9	3
3	4	9	7	2	6	1	5	8
5	3	4	2	1	7	6	8	9
9	2	8	4	6	3	5	7	1
7	6	1	9	8	5	3	2	4

109

7	5	2	4	8	3	1	9	6
3	8	6	2	9	1	7	5	4
1	9	4	6	5	7	2	8	3
5	7	8	1	3	2	6	4	9
6	1	9	5	7	4	8	3	2
4	2	3	9	6	8	5	1	7
8	4	7	3	1	6	9	2	5
2	6	5	8	4	9	3	7	1
9	3	1	7	2	5	4	6	8

110

3	1	2	5	6	4	9	8	7
5	8	7	9	3	1	4	6	2
6	9	4	7	8	2	5	3	1
4	6	3	8	2	7	1	5	9
9	5	8	1	4	6	7	2	3
2	7	1	3	9	5	8	4	6
7	2	5	6	1	8	3	9	4
1	3	6	4	5	9	2	7	8
8	4	9	2	7	3	6	1	5

111

1	9	4	2	3	8	7	6	5
2	6	3	1	7	5	8	4	9
7	8	5	4	6	9	1	3	2
9	1	2	8	5	3	4	7	6
3	7	6	9	4	1	2	5	8
4	5	8	6	2	7	9	1	3
8	2	7	3	1	6	5	9	4
5	3	9	7	8	4	6	2	1
6	4	1	5	9	2	3	8	7

112

8	7	5	3	6	1	2	9	4
9	2	4	8	5	7	6	3	1
1	3	6	2	9	4	5	8	7
7	1	2	4	3	5	8	6	9
6	5	3	9	1	8	4	7	2
4	8	9	6	7	2	1	5	3
2	9	1	5	8	3	7	4	6
5	6	7	1	4	9	3	2	8
3	4	8	7	2	6	9	1	5

13

9	6	5	4	7	3	8	1	2
4	2	3	1	6	8	5	9	7
7	1	8	2	5	9	4	6	3
5	9	4	3	1	6	7	2	8
3	8	2	9	4	7	1	5	6
1	7	6	8	2	5	3	4	9
2	5	9	7	3	1	6	8	4
6	4	7	5	8	2	9	3	1
8	3	1	6	9	4	2	7	5

14

1	9	7	2	8	6	4	5	3
6	3	5	4	1	9	7	8	2
8	2	4	5	7	3	9	1	6
2	1	3	8	5	4	6	9	7
5	7	9	1	6	2	8	3	4
4	6	8	3	9	7	1	2	5
7	4	1	9	3	5	2	6	8
9	5	6	7	2	8	3	4	1
3	8	2	6	4	1	5	7	9

15

8	6	9	2	1	4	7	5	3
2	5	3	9	8	7	6	4	1
7	4	1	6	3	5	2	9	8
4	8	5	7	9	6	1	3	2
9	3	7	4	2	1	5	8	6
6	1	2	3	5	8	9	7	4
1	7	6	8	4	9	3	2	5
5	2	4	1	7	3	8	6	9
3	9	8	5	6	2	4	1	7

16

8	1	2	4	6	9	7	3	5
7	3	4	8	5	2	6	1	9
5	9	6	3	7	1	4	2	8
9	6	5	2	4	8	1	7	3
4	2	1	7	9	3	8	5	6
3	8	7	5	1	6	2	9	4
1	5	3	6	2	4	9	8	7
6	7	9	1	8	5	3	4	2
2	4	8	9	3	7	5	6	1

17

6	7	1	3	2	5	9	4	8
3	9	5	6	4	8	2	7	1
2	8	4	1	7	9	3	5	6
4	3	2	8	1	7	5	6	9
1	6	7	5	9	4	8	3	2
8	5	9	2	6	3	4	1	7
5	4	6	9	8	1	7	2	3
7	1	8	4	3	2	6	9	5
9	2	3	7	5	6	1	8	4

18

2	7	9	1	5	8	4	3	6
1	6	4	3	2	7	5	9	8
3	8	5	4	6	9	2	7	1
9	5	2	6	7	3	8	1	4
4	3	7	8	1	5	6	2	9
8	1	6	9	4	2	7	5	3
6	2	3	5	8	1	9	4	7
5	4	1	7	9	6	3	8	2
7	9	8	2	3	4	1	6	5

19

1	5	3	9	2	8	6	4	7
6	9	7	5	1	4	8	2	3
2	4	8	6	3	7	9	1	5
9	8	4	3	7	6	1	5	2
3	2	1	4	9	5	7	6	8
7	6	5	2	8	1	4	3	9
4	1	9	7	5	3	2	8	6
5	7	6	8	4	2	3	9	1
8	3	2	1	6	9	5	7	4

20

1	6	2	8	9	5	7	3	4
3	5	4	6	7	2	9	1	8
7	9	8	1	4	3	2	5	6
2	7	6	3	5	4	8	9	1
9	8	3	2	6	1	5	4	7
4	1	5	7	8	9	6	2	3
5	4	7	9	3	8	1	6	2
8	2	9	4	1	6	3	7	5
6	3	1	5	2	7	4	8	9

Puzzle 121

5	1	9	6	4	7	2	3	8
2	6	7	5	8	3	4	9	1
4	3	8	1	2	9	7	5	6
6	9	1	3	5	2	8	4	7
7	2	4	9	1	8	5	6	3
3	8	5	7	6	4	9	1	2
1	5	2	8	9	6	3	7	4
9	4	3	2	7	1	6	8	5
8	7	6	4	3	5	1	2	9

Puzzle 122

8	1	3	7	6	2	4	9	5
6	5	7	3	4	9	1	8	2
4	9	2	1	8	5	6	7	3
9	8	6	2	5	4	3	1	7
1	2	4	6	7	3	8	5	9
3	7	5	9	1	8	2	4	6
7	6	9	8	3	1	5	2	4
2	4	8	5	9	6	7	3	1
5	3	1	4	2	7	9	6	8

Puzzle 123

3	8	2	9	1	5	4	6	7
6	9	5	2	4	7	8	1	3
4	7	1	3	8	6	5	9	2
1	4	6	5	7	9	2	3	8
5	3	8	6	2	4	1	7	9
7	2	9	1	3	8	6	4	5
9	6	7	8	5	1	3	2	4
8	1	3	4	9	2	7	5	6
2	5	4	7	6	3	9	8	1

Puzzle 124

8	1	9	4	7	2	6	5	3
2	5	6	9	8	3	1	4	7
7	4	3	1	6	5	8	9	2
3	8	4	2	1	7	5	6	9
6	7	2	8	5	9	3	1	4
5	9	1	3	4	6	7	2	8
9	6	7	5	3	4	2	8	1
1	2	5	7	9	8	4	3	6
4	3	8	6	2	1	9	7	5

Puzzle 125

6	4	8	7	3	1	9	5	2
9	5	1	2	4	8	7	6	3
7	3	2	6	9	5	4	8	1
8	6	7	3	2	4	5	1	9
5	9	4	8	1	6	2	3	7
1	2	3	5	7	9	8	4	6
3	7	5	1	8	2	6	9	4
2	8	9	4	6	3	1	7	5
4	1	6	9	5	7	3	2	8

Puzzle 126

7	8	3	4	2	6	1	5	9
5	4	6	7	1	9	8	2	3
9	1	2	3	5	8	6	7	4
6	9	1	2	8	4	7	3	5
4	5	8	9	3	7	2	6	1
3	2	7	5	6	1	9	4	8
1	7	9	6	4	3	5	8	2
2	6	4	8	9	5	3	1	7
8	3	5	1	7	2	4	9	6

Puzzle 127

7	1	2	4	3	9	8	5	6
3	5	8	6	2	1	4	9	7
9	6	4	5	8	7	3	1	2
6	4	1	2	9	5	7	8	3
8	3	7	1	4	6	5	2	9
5	2	9	3	7	8	1	6	4
4	8	3	9	5	2	6	7	1
2	7	6	8	1	3	9	4	5
1	9	5	7	6	4	2	3	8

Puzzle 128

1	6	3	7	4	5	8	9	2
4	9	7	1	2	8	6	5	3
2	8	5	6	3	9	4	1	7
5	7	1	4	6	2	3	8	9
3	2	8	5	9	7	1	6	4
9	4	6	8	1	3	7	2	5
6	3	2	9	7	1	5	4	8
8	1	9	3	5	4	2	7	6
7	5	4	2	8	6	9	3	1

129

8	5	9	3	6	7	1	4	2
3	1	4	8	9	2	7	5	6
6	7	2	1	5	4	8	9	3
9	8	3	6	2	1	5	7	4
2	6	7	5	4	9	3	1	8
5	4	1	7	3	8	2	6	9
4	3	5	2	1	6	9	8	7
1	9	8	4	7	3	6	2	5
7	2	6	9	8	5	4	3	1

130

8	7	9	1	5	2	3	4	6
5	4	1	8	6	3	7	2	9
2	3	6	7	4	9	5	8	1
3	9	8	5	2	7	6	1	4
1	5	7	4	9	6	8	3	2
4	6	2	3	1	8	9	5	7
7	2	3	9	8	1	4	6	5
6	8	5	2	7	4	1	9	3
9	1	4	6	3	5	2	7	8

131

7	5	4	3	8	9	6	1	2
1	2	6	5	4	7	3	9	8
9	8	3	2	6	1	4	5	7
4	9	8	7	5	2	1	3	6
5	1	7	4	3	6	8	2	9
6	3	2	1	9	8	7	4	5
3	7	1	8	2	5	9	6	4
2	4	9	6	7	3	5	8	1
8	6	5	9	1	4	2	7	3

132

1	9	7	5	6	4	8	3	2
6	2	5	9	3	8	4	1	7
4	8	3	2	1	7	9	5	6
9	5	1	8	2	6	7	4	3
8	4	2	1	7	3	5	6	9
7	3	6	4	9	5	2	8	1
5	6	9	3	4	2	1	7	8
2	7	4	6	8	1	3	9	5
3	1	8	7	5	9	6	2	4

133

4	5	8	3	2	6	7	9	1
7	1	9	4	8	5	6	3	2
6	3	2	1	7	9	5	4	8
5	9	1	7	3	2	4	8	6
2	6	3	9	4	8	1	5	7
8	4	7	6	5	1	3	2	9
9	8	4	5	6	7	2	1	3
3	2	6	8	1	4	9	7	5
1	7	5	2	9	3	8	6	4

134

6	8	7	3	4	1	5	9	2
5	3	1	9	8	2	6	4	7
2	9	4	5	6	7	1	3	8
7	6	9	1	5	8	4	2	3
1	4	2	6	3	9	8	7	5
3	5	8	2	7	4	9	6	1
8	7	3	4	1	6	2	5	9
4	2	5	8	9	3	7	1	6
9	1	6	7	2	5	3	8	4

135

1	6	9	5	4	7	8	3	2
5	8	3	6	2	9	7	1	4
4	2	7	8	3	1	6	5	9
7	3	6	9	5	2	1	4	8
9	1	4	7	6	8	3	2	5
8	5	2	3	1	4	9	7	6
6	4	8	2	7	3	5	9	1
2	7	5	1	9	6	4	8	3
3	9	1	4	8	5	2	6	7

136

2	8	7	4	5	1	9	3	6
4	5	9	8	3	6	7	2	1
3	1	6	9	7	2	8	4	5
6	2	8	3	4	7	1	5	9
1	4	5	2	6	9	3	7	8
7	9	3	5	1	8	4	6	2
8	3	2	7	9	5	6	1	4
9	6	4	1	2	3	5	8	7
5	7	1	6	8	4	2	9	3

9	5	6	1	3	4	8	7	2
2	1	8	5	7	9	6	4	3
7	3	4	8	2	6	5	9	1
8	2	5	6	9	3	7	1	4
1	9	3	7	4	5	2	6	8
6	4	7	2	8	1	3	5	9
5	7	2	4	1	8	9	3	6
3	8	1	9	6	7	4	2	5
4	6	9	3	5	2	1	8	7

5	1	8	9	4	2	3	6	7
4	9	7	3	6	8	2	1	5
2	3	6	5	1	7	4	8	9
7	4	2	1	9	5	8	3	6
3	6	1	7	8	4	9	5	2
8	5	9	2	3	6	1	7	4
9	7	4	8	5	3	6	2	1
6	2	3	4	7	1	5	9	8
1	8	5	6	2	9	7	4	3

9	6	3	4	5	8	1	7	2
4	8	5	1	7	2	6	3	9
7	1	2	3	6	9	5	4	8
2	3	1	5	4	6	8	9	7
8	9	4	2	1	7	3	5	6
6	5	7	9	8	3	2	1	4
1	7	9	6	2	5	4	8	3
3	4	6	8	9	1	7	2	5
5	2	8	7	3	4	9	6	1

2	6	4	5	9	8	7	3	1
9	1	8	3	7	2	4	6	5
3	7	5	6	1	4	2	9	8
6	8	9	1	2	7	3	5	4
7	5	3	9	4	6	1	8	2
4	2	1	8	3	5	9	7	6
5	4	7	2	8	3	6	1	9
8	9	2	7	6	1	5	4	3
1	3	6	4	5	9	8	2	7

5	7	2	4	9	3	8	1	6
3	1	6	8	7	5	9	4	2
9	8	4	6	2	1	3	5	7
1	3	5	2	6	8	7	9	4
7	4	8	3	1	9	2	6	5
2	6	9	7	5	4	1	8	3
6	2	1	5	8	7	4	3	9
4	9	7	1	3	6	5	2	8
8	5	3	9	4	2	6	7	1

9	2	4	1	6	3	5	8	7
5	7	8	4	2	9	1	6	3
1	6	3	7	8	5	2	4	9
8	3	1	2	4	6	9	7	5
2	4	5	3	9	7	6	1	8
7	9	6	8	5	1	4	3	2
3	8	2	5	1	4	7	9	6
4	5	9	6	7	8	3	2	1
6	1	7	9	3	2	8	5	4

9	2	1	4	3	5	8	7	6
6	8	3	7	2	1	5	9	4
7	5	4	8	6	9	2	1	3
5	1	6	3	4	8	7	2	9
3	9	8	2	5	7	6	4	1
4	7	2	9	1	6	3	5	8
2	3	5	1	8	4	9	6	7
8	4	9	6	7	2	1	3	5
1	6	7	5	9	3	4	8	2

3	7	8	5	2	9	4	1	6
9	2	6	3	1	4	7	8	5
1	4	5	8	7	6	3	2	9
8	3	1	9	5	2	6	7	4
6	9	2	1	4	7	5	3	8
4	5	7	6	3	8	1	9	2
2	1	3	4	9	5	8	6	7
5	8	9	7	6	3	2	4	1
7	6	4	2	8	1	9	5	3

145

7	6	2	4	9	8	3	1	5
9	5	1	7	6	3	8	2	4
3	4	8	5	2	1	7	6	9
8	3	9	2	5	4	6	7	1
5	1	6	9	8	7	4	3	2
4	2	7	1	3	6	9	5	8
6	7	4	8	1	2	5	9	3
1	8	5	3	7	9	2	4	6
2	9	3	6	4	5	1	8	7

146

9	7	4	1	2	3	6	8	5
3	6	8	9	7	5	2	1	4
2	5	1	6	8	4	9	7	3
8	4	7	3	6	2	1	5	9
6	3	9	4	5	1	7	2	8
5	1	2	7	9	8	3	4	6
4	8	3	2	1	6	5	9	7
7	2	5	8	3	9	4	6	1
1	9	6	5	4	7	8	3	2

147

9	1	8	3	6	5	4	2	7
4	5	6	9	7	2	1	3	8
7	3	2	4	8	1	6	9	5
5	4	3	1	9	8	7	6	2
6	7	1	2	5	4	9	8	3
2	8	9	6	3	7	5	1	4
8	6	7	5	1	3	2	4	9
3	9	4	7	2	6	8	5	1
1	2	5	8	4	9	3	7	6

148

2	3	8	7	9	1	6	4	5
5	6	4	2	8	3	9	1	7
1	7	9	4	6	5	2	8	3
6	8	3	5	2	7	1	9	4
4	9	2	1	3	6	5	7	8
7	1	5	9	4	8	3	6	2
8	5	6	3	7	9	4	2	1
3	2	7	6	1	4	8	5	9
9	4	1	8	5	2	7	3	6

149

7	5	8	6	4	3	1	9	2
3	2	9	1	8	5	7	6	4
4	6	1	2	7	9	8	3	5
9	4	7	5	6	1	2	8	3
2	1	6	7	3	8	4	5	9
8	3	5	4	9	2	6	1	7
6	7	3	8	5	4	9	2	1
5	8	2	9	1	7	3	4	6
1	9	4	3	2	6	5	7	8

150

3	1	6	5	7	4	2	9	8
8	5	2	9	3	6	4	1	7
4	9	7	2	8	1	3	5	6
6	3	5	7	4	8	9	2	1
2	4	9	6	1	5	8	7	3
7	8	1	3	9	2	6	4	5
5	2	8	1	6	9	7	3	4
1	6	3	4	2	7	5	8	9
9	7	4	8	5	3	1	6	2

151

6	9	2	5	4	3	8	7	1
4	3	7	8	1	9	5	6	2
8	5	1	7	2	6	4	3	9
9	2	6	4	8	5	3	1	7
3	7	4	1	6	2	9	8	5
1	8	5	3	9	7	2	4	6
2	6	8	9	7	4	1	5	3
5	4	9	6	3	1	7	2	8
7	1	3	2	5	8	6	9	4

152

2	5	8	3	4	7	9	6	1
1	7	9	6	5	8	3	4	2
4	3	6	9	1	2	5	8	7
7	1	4	2	8	3	6	5	9
3	9	2	4	6	5	1	7	8
6	8	5	7	9	1	4	2	3
9	6	1	8	7	4	2	3	5
5	2	7	1	3	6	8	9	4
8	4	3	5	2	9	7	1	6

153

1	9	7	4	8	3	6	2	5
3	8	4	6	5	2	7	1	9
2	6	5	7	1	9	8	3	4
7	4	1	5	2	8	3	9	6
6	2	3	1	9	4	5	7	8
9	5	8	3	7	6	2	4	1
8	3	9	2	6	1	4	5	7
4	7	6	9	3	5	1	8	2
5	1	2	8	4	7	9	6	3

154

7	6	3	5	9	4	8	2	1
2	4	8	6	3	1	5	9	7
1	9	5	2	7	8	6	3	4
5	3	4	8	1	9	2	7	6
8	7	6	4	2	3	1	5	9
9	1	2	7	5	6	3	4	8
6	2	9	1	4	5	7	8	3
3	8	7	9	6	2	4	1	5
4	5	1	3	8	7	9	6	2

155

8	3	5	6	2	9	4	7	1
4	2	1	8	7	3	6	5	9
6	7	9	5	1	4	3	8	2
3	6	4	7	8	2	1	9	5
9	5	8	4	3	1	7	2	6
2	1	7	9	6	5	8	4	3
1	8	3	2	5	7	9	6	4
5	4	6	1	9	8	2	3	7
7	9	2	3	4	6	5	1	8

156

1	7	8	3	9	6	4	5	2
5	2	4	8	1	7	6	9	3
3	6	9	4	2	5	8	1	7
8	9	7	6	3	2	5	4	1
4	1	3	9	5	8	2	7	6
2	5	6	1	7	4	9	3	8
7	8	5	2	4	3	1	6	9
9	3	2	5	6	1	7	8	4
6	4	1	7	8	9	3	2	5

157

1	9	5	6	3	8	2	4	7
3	7	4	9	5	2	1	8	6
8	6	2	7	4	1	5	9	3
9	2	1	8	7	4	3	6	5
4	5	8	1	6	3	7	2	9
7	3	6	2	9	5	4	1	8
5	8	7	4	2	9	6	3	1
6	4	9	3	1	7	8	5	2
2	1	3	5	8	6	9	7	4

158

6	9	8	2	1	3	7	4	5
1	7	4	5	8	6	3	9	2
3	2	5	9	4	7	6	8	1
8	5	2	4	7	9	1	3	6
9	3	7	6	2	1	8	5	4
4	1	6	8	3	5	9	2	7
7	8	1	3	5	2	4	6	9
5	4	9	7	6	8	2	1	3
2	6	3	1	9	4	5	7	8

159

3	8	9	5	4	7	1	2	6
4	5	7	1	6	2	3	8	9
1	6	2	9	8	3	4	7	5
7	9	1	8	3	6	5	4	2
8	2	4	7	1	5	9	6	3
5	3	6	4	2	9	8	1	7
9	1	5	2	7	4	6	3	8
2	4	3	6	9	8	7	5	1
6	7	8	3	5	1	2	9	4

160

7	3	6	5	8	2	4	1	9
9	8	5	3	1	4	2	6	7
2	1	4	6	9	7	8	5	3
6	7	8	9	3	1	5	4	2
5	2	1	7	4	8	3	9	6
3	4	9	2	6	5	1	7	8
1	5	7	8	2	9	6	3	4
4	6	2	1	7	3	9	8	5
8	9	3	4	5	6	7	2	1

161

4	8	2	6	1	7	3	9	5
3	5	6	9	4	2	8	1	7
1	9	7	5	8	3	4	6	2
6	4	9	7	2	8	1	5	3
5	3	8	4	6	1	2	7	9
2	7	1	3	5	9	6	4	8
8	1	5	2	9	6	7	3	4
9	2	3	1	7	4	5	8	6
7	6	4	8	3	5	9	2	1

162

6	7	2	1	4	3	9	5	8
4	3	5	2	8	9	6	7	1
9	8	1	7	5	6	4	2	3
3	1	8	5	9	4	2	6	7
2	4	6	3	7	8	5	1	9
7	5	9	6	2	1	8	3	4
5	6	4	9	1	7	3	8	2
8	2	7	4	3	5	1	9	6
1	9	3	8	6	2	7	4	5

163

8	9	2	7	1	5	3	6	4
7	1	4	3	6	2	8	9	5
6	3	5	8	4	9	2	7	1
5	4	8	9	3	1	6	2	7
3	7	6	4	2	8	1	5	9
1	2	9	5	7	6	4	8	3
4	5	3	2	8	7	9	1	6
9	8	1	6	5	3	7	4	2
2	6	7	1	9	4	5	3	8

164

9	5	3	1	8	4	7	6	2
2	8	4	7	9	6	3	5	1
6	1	7	3	2	5	4	8	9
7	3	5	2	1	9	8	4	6
4	9	2	6	3	8	1	7	5
8	6	1	5	4	7	9	2	3
5	2	8	9	7	3	6	1	4
1	4	9	8	6	2	5	3	7
3	7	6	4	5	1	2	9	8

165

8	6	3	2	5	1	9	7	4
7	4	1	3	9	6	2	8	5
2	5	9	7	8	4	1	3	6
9	1	6	8	4	7	3	5	2
5	2	7	6	3	9	4	1	8
3	8	4	5	1	2	6	9	7
4	3	8	1	6	5	7	2	9
6	7	5	9	2	3	8	4	1
1	9	2	4	7	8	5	6	3

166

5	4	3	2	1	7	8	6	9
6	8	1	3	9	5	2	4	7
7	2	9	8	4	6	5	1	3
3	6	7	5	8	2	4	9	1
1	5	4	9	6	3	7	8	2
8	9	2	1	7	4	6	3	5
9	7	6	4	2	1	3	5	8
4	1	5	7	3	8	9	2	6
2	3	8	6	5	9	1	7	4

167

9	4	7	1	5	2	6	8	3
1	2	8	9	6	3	4	7	5
3	6	5	4	7	8	1	9	2
6	5	3	2	1	7	9	4	8
4	1	9	5	8	6	2	3	7
7	8	2	3	9	4	5	1	6
5	9	6	8	3	1	7	2	4
2	3	1	7	4	5	8	6	9
8	7	4	6	2	9	3	5	1

168

8	3	5	2	7	6	4	9	1
1	9	2	5	8	4	6	7	3
6	4	7	1	9	3	2	8	5
7	6	9	8	4	1	3	5	2
3	8	4	9	2	5	7	1	6
5	2	1	6	3	7	8	4	9
9	7	3	4	5	2	1	6	8
4	1	8	3	6	9	5	2	7
2	5	6	7	1	8	9	3	4

169

5	7	6	8	2	1	9	4	3
8	1	3	5	9	4	6	7	2
9	2	4	3	7	6	5	1	8
6	8	9	4	3	5	1	2	7
4	5	7	2	1	8	3	6	9
2	3	1	9	6	7	8	5	4
1	9	5	7	4	3	2	8	6
3	4	8	6	5	2	7	9	1
7	6	2	1	8	9	4	3	5

170

1	3	7	5	4	9	6	2	8
4	5	6	3	8	2	9	1	7
8	9	2	6	1	7	4	5	3
9	4	1	7	6	5	3	8	2
6	2	3	8	9	1	5	7	4
5	7	8	2	3	4	1	6	9
7	8	9	1	5	3	2	4	6
2	1	4	9	7	6	8	3	5
3	6	5	4	2	8	7	9	1

171

4	2	3	6	7	9	8	5	1
9	7	8	1	3	5	4	2	6
5	1	6	2	4	8	9	3	7
8	5	4	7	1	3	2	6	9
6	9	1	5	8	2	3	7	4
7	3	2	9	6	4	5	1	8
1	4	9	3	5	6	7	8	2
3	8	7	4	2	1	6	9	5
2	6	5	8	9	7	1	4	3

172

2	6	4	7	3	8	1	9	5
3	1	7	9	4	5	2	6	8
9	5	8	1	2	6	3	7	4
8	7	6	3	9	4	5	1	2
4	2	9	5	1	7	6	8	3
1	3	5	6	8	2	9	4	7
7	4	3	2	6	1	8	5	9
6	8	2	4	5	9	7	3	1
5	9	1	8	7	3	4	2	6

173

5	8	3	7	4	9	2	1	6
6	9	2	3	1	8	5	7	4
4	7	1	2	5	6	8	9	3
7	1	4	8	9	3	6	5	2
9	5	8	1	6	2	4	3	7
2	3	6	5	7	4	9	8	1
1	4	9	6	8	7	3	2	5
8	2	5	4	3	1	7	6	9
3	6	7	9	2	5	1	4	8

174

3	2	4	7	9	5	8	1	6
1	7	8	6	4	3	5	9	2
5	9	6	8	2	1	7	3	4
2	5	7	3	8	6	1	4	9
4	3	9	5	1	2	6	8	7
6	8	1	9	7	4	3	2	5
7	1	3	2	6	9	4	5	8
9	6	5	4	3	8	2	7	1
8	4	2	1	5	7	9	6	3

175

3	2	4	9	7	5	1	8	6
5	1	7	8	2	6	9	3	4
6	8	9	4	3	1	2	7	5
4	7	3	2	6	8	5	9	1
1	5	8	3	9	4	6	2	7
9	6	2	1	5	7	8	4	3
2	9	5	7	1	3	4	6	8
7	4	1	6	8	2	3	5	9
8	3	6	5	4	9	7	1	2

176

9	5	1	2	6	3	8	4	7
2	3	6	8	7	4	1	5	9
4	8	7	9	5	1	6	3	2
6	2	9	4	1	5	7	8	3
7	1	8	3	9	6	4	2	5
3	4	5	7	8	2	9	6	1
5	7	2	1	4	8	3	9	6
1	6	4	5	3	9	2	7	8
8	9	3	6	2	7	5	1	4

177

5	8	9	7	6	1	2	3	4
1	6	7	3	4	2	8	5	9
4	2	3	8	5	9	1	7	6
7	1	2	6	3	4	5	9	8
6	9	4	1	8	5	3	2	7
8	3	5	9	2	7	6	4	1
3	5	1	4	9	8	7	6	2
9	7	6	2	1	3	4	8	5
2	4	8	5	7	6	9	1	3

178

2	6	5	7	8	9	1	3	4
4	8	7	1	6	3	5	9	2
9	3	1	2	4	5	7	6	8
3	2	8	4	5	6	9	7	1
5	4	9	3	7	1	8	2	6
7	1	6	9	2	8	3	4	5
1	5	2	6	3	7	4	8	9
8	7	4	5	9	2	6	1	3
6	9	3	8	1	4	2	5	7

179

3	7	1	5	2	9	4	8	6
2	4	8	3	7	6	1	9	5
6	9	5	8	1	4	3	7	2
5	1	3	9	4	7	2	6	8
7	2	9	1	6	8	5	3	4
8	6	4	2	3	5	9	1	7
4	5	6	7	9	1	8	2	3
9	3	7	4	8	2	6	5	1
1	8	2	6	5	3	7	4	9

180

8	3	4	6	2	9	5	7	1
2	1	5	8	4	7	6	9	3
7	9	6	3	1	5	4	8	2
1	5	2	9	8	3	7	6	4
9	7	8	1	6	4	2	3	5
4	6	3	5	7	2	8	1	9
5	8	9	2	3	6	1	4	7
6	2	7	4	9	1	3	5	8
3	4	1	7	5	8	9	2	6

181

3	7	4	5	6	1	2	9	8
9	8	2	7	3	4	5	6	1
1	6	5	8	9	2	3	7	4
5	3	9	4	8	7	6	1	2
7	4	1	2	5	6	9	8	3
8	2	6	3	1	9	7	4	5
6	9	8	1	2	5	4	3	7
2	1	7	6	4	3	8	5	9
4	5	3	9	7	8	1	2	6

182

2	9	4	8	5	3	7	1	6
1	5	8	6	9	7	2	4	3
3	7	6	1	2	4	9	5	8
7	3	5	2	4	9	6	8	1
8	1	2	3	6	5	4	7	9
4	6	9	7	1	8	5	3	2
5	4	1	9	3	6	8	2	7
9	8	3	5	7	2	1	6	4
6	2	7	4	8	1	3	9	5

183

9	8	7	3	5	2	4	6	1
1	6	3	9	7	4	8	2	5
5	4	2	8	1	6	7	9	3
4	2	9	7	6	3	1	5	8
8	1	5	2	4	9	6	3	7
3	7	6	5	8	1	2	4	9
6	5	4	1	9	8	3	7	2
7	3	8	4	2	5	9	1	6
2	9	1	6	3	7	5	8	4

184

6	9	8	3	1	2	7	5	4
7	4	2	5	6	9	3	1	8
1	5	3	7	4	8	2	9	6
4	8	9	2	3	5	1	6	7
5	2	7	1	9	6	4	8	3
3	6	1	8	7	4	5	2	9
8	3	6	4	5	1	9	7	2
9	1	4	6	2	7	8	3	5
2	7	5	9	8	3	6	4	1

185

4	5	6	3	2	1	7	8	9
8	3	1	6	7	9	2	4	5
7	2	9	4	5	8	1	6	3
1	8	2	9	4	7	3	5	6
6	7	5	2	8	3	9	1	4
3	9	4	5	1	6	8	2	7
9	4	8	1	3	5	6	7	2
2	1	3	7	6	4	5	9	8
5	6	7	8	9	2	4	3	1

186

4	2	3	5	9	8	1	6	7
7	6	9	4	2	1	8	3	5
1	8	5	3	6	7	4	2	9
6	3	4	9	7	5	2	8	1
5	9	2	8	1	6	3	7	4
8	1	7	2	3	4	9	5	6
3	7	1	6	8	9	5	4	2
9	4	8	7	5	2	6	1	3
2	5	6	1	4	3	7	9	8

187

8	4	1	9	2	6	3	7	5
5	9	3	1	4	7	2	8	6
2	7	6	3	5	8	4	9	1
9	8	7	4	3	1	6	5	2
1	6	5	2	7	9	8	3	4
4	3	2	8	6	5	7	1	9
3	1	8	6	9	4	5	2	7
6	5	9	7	8	2	1	4	3
7	2	4	5	1	3	9	6	8

188

6	9	2	8	7	1	3	5	4
7	5	8	3	4	6	1	9	2
3	1	4	2	5	9	6	8	7
4	8	6	5	9	2	7	3	1
5	2	9	1	3	7	4	6	8
1	7	3	4	6	8	9	2	5
8	6	7	9	1	5	2	4	3
2	4	1	6	8	3	5	7	9
9	3	5	7	2	4	8	1	6

189

2	7	4	9	1	8	3	5	6
1	6	8	7	3	5	9	2	4
9	3	5	6	4	2	7	8	1
7	4	2	1	6	9	5	3	8
5	8	9	4	2	3	6	1	7
3	1	6	8	5	7	4	9	2
6	2	3	5	8	4	1	7	9
8	9	1	3	7	6	2	4	5
4	5	7	2	9	1	8	6	3

190

4	6	3	2	8	5	1	9	7
9	2	5	1	3	7	4	8	6
1	7	8	6	9	4	5	3	2
2	3	6	4	5	8	9	7	1
5	8	9	7	1	6	3	2	4
7	4	1	9	2	3	8	6	5
8	5	2	3	7	1	6	4	9
6	1	7	8	4	9	2	5	3
3	9	4	5	6	2	7	1	8

191

8	3	2	6	7	9	5	1	4
5	4	1	3	8	2	6	9	7
7	9	6	1	4	5	8	2	3
2	5	4	7	9	1	3	6	8
1	6	7	2	3	8	9	4	5
9	8	3	5	6	4	1	7	2
6	7	5	9	2	3	4	8	1
3	2	8	4	1	6	7	5	9
4	1	9	8	5	7	2	3	6

192

6	9	2	1	5	3	4	7	8
4	1	7	6	2	8	9	3	5
8	3	5	7	4	9	2	6	1
7	4	9	5	1	6	3	8	2
3	6	8	2	9	7	5	1	4
2	5	1	8	3	4	6	9	7
1	2	3	9	8	5	7	4	6
9	8	6	4	7	2	1	5	3
5	7	4	3	6	1	8	2	9

193

6	2	8	5	4	1	9	7	3
4	5	7	6	3	9	8	1	2
9	1	3	8	2	7	6	5	4
3	4	1	9	5	2	7	8	6
8	7	2	4	1	6	5	3	9
5	6	9	3	7	8	4	2	1
1	8	4	2	9	5	3	6	7
2	9	6	7	8	3	1	4	5
7	3	5	1	6	4	2	9	8

194

9	7	2	8	1	5	6	3	4
4	3	6	7	9	2	1	5	8
5	1	8	3	4	6	7	2	9
3	4	5	2	8	1	9	7	6
2	8	9	6	7	4	5	1	3
1	6	7	9	5	3	8	4	2
7	9	3	1	2	8	4	6	5
8	2	4	5	6	7	3	9	1
6	5	1	4	3	9	2	8	7

195

8	6	2	9	3	1	7	4	5
4	1	9	8	7	5	2	3	6
3	7	5	2	4	6	9	1	8
6	4	3	1	2	8	5	9	7
7	9	1	6	5	3	4	8	2
2	5	8	4	9	7	1	6	3
5	3	4	7	8	9	6	2	1
1	2	7	3	6	4	8	5	9
9	8	6	5	1	2	3	7	4

196

5	1	4	6	8	2	3	9	7
7	8	3	5	4	9	2	6	1
2	9	6	3	7	1	5	4	8
6	5	1	8	3	4	9	7	2
4	2	8	1	9	7	6	5	3
9	3	7	2	6	5	8	1	4
1	4	2	9	5	3	7	8	6
3	6	9	7	1	8	4	2	5
8	7	5	4	2	6	1	3	9

197

8	5	3	6	7	2	1	4	9
2	7	1	9	3	4	8	6	5
6	4	9	5	8	1	7	3	2
1	9	4	2	5	7	6	8	3
7	8	5	3	1	6	2	9	4
3	6	2	4	9	8	5	1	7
4	2	8	7	6	9	3	5	1
5	1	7	8	4	3	9	2	6
9	3	6	1	2	5	4	7	8

198

4	6	8	1	3	7	2	9	5
3	5	1	8	9	2	4	6	7
9	7	2	5	6	4	8	3	1
2	8	3	7	5	6	1	4	9
5	9	6	4	2	1	3	7	8
7	1	4	9	8	3	6	5	2
8	4	7	6	1	5	9	2	3
1	2	5	3	4	9	7	8	6
6	3	9	2	7	8	5	1	4

199

3	2	5	9	4	1	7	6	8
6	4	1	3	8	7	9	2	5
8	7	9	5	2	6	4	1	3
4	1	6	7	3	9	5	8	2
5	8	7	2	6	4	1	3	9
9	3	2	1	5	8	6	7	4
7	5	3	6	9	2	8	4	1
2	6	4	8	1	5	3	9	7
1	9	8	4	7	3	2	5	6

200

2	9	7	8	1	5	3	6	4
5	6	8	7	4	3	1	2	9
4	1	3	6	9	2	5	8	7
8	3	6	1	2	7	4	9	5
9	4	5	3	6	8	7	1	2
1	7	2	9	5	4	6	3	8
3	5	4	2	8	1	9	7	6
6	2	1	5	7	9	8	4	3
7	8	9	4	3	6	2	5	1

201

1	5	8	3	9	2	4	6	7
6	3	4	7	5	8	1	9	2
7	9	2	1	4	6	8	3	5
2	4	1	5	7	3	9	8	6
9	7	5	8	6	1	3	2	4
3	8	6	9	2	4	7	5	1
5	1	7	2	8	9	6	4	3
8	6	3	4	1	5	2	7	9
4	2	9	6	3	7	5	1	8

202

1	5	8	2	7	9	6	3	4
7	3	2	1	4	6	5	9	8
4	9	6	5	3	8	7	1	2
8	4	7	3	2	5	9	6	1
3	2	9	8	6	1	4	5	7
6	1	5	7	9	4	8	2	3
5	6	1	4	8	3	2	7	9
2	8	3	9	5	7	1	4	6
9	7	4	6	1	2	3	8	5

203

6	4	9	8	5	1	3	2	7
7	1	5	3	4	2	6	8	9
3	2	8	9	6	7	1	5	4
4	3	1	5	2	8	9	7	6
9	5	2	4	7	6	8	1	3
8	6	7	1	3	9	5	4	2
5	7	3	6	1	4	2	9	8
2	8	6	7	9	5	4	3	1
1	9	4	2	8	3	7	6	5

204

6	4	8	9	1	7	2	5	3
1	2	7	6	5	3	8	4	9
5	9	3	8	4	2	1	7	6
4	8	6	1	3	9	5	2	7
9	3	2	4	7	5	6	1	8
7	5	1	2	6	8	3	9	4
2	1	9	3	8	4	7	6	5
3	7	4	5	2	6	9	8	1
8	6	5	7	9	1	4	3	2

205

9	4	3	2	5	6	7	1	8
5	2	7	1	3	8	9	4	6
6	1	8	4	7	9	2	5	3
8	3	4	7	1	5	6	2	9
2	5	6	9	8	3	1	7	4
7	9	1	6	2	4	3	8	5
3	8	2	5	6	1	4	9	7
4	7	5	3	9	2	8	6	1
1	6	9	8	4	7	5	3	2

206

8	4	9	5	6	7	2	3	1
6	3	7	8	2	1	5	4	9
5	2	1	3	4	9	7	6	8
7	5	6	4	8	2	1	9	3
1	9	4	6	7	3	8	5	2
2	8	3	9	1	5	4	7	6
9	1	5	7	3	8	6	2	4
4	7	2	1	9	6	3	8	5
3	6	8	2	5	4	9	1	7

207

7	1	8	3	2	5	9	4	6
9	4	6	8	1	7	5	3	2
2	3	5	9	6	4	1	8	7
4	8	3	2	7	9	6	5	1
1	2	9	4	5	6	8	7	3
6	5	7	1	8	3	2	9	4
8	6	4	7	9	1	3	2	5
5	7	2	6	3	8	4	1	9
3	9	1	5	4	2	7	6	8

208

8	5	2	4	7	6	3	1	9
7	6	9	5	3	1	4	2	8
4	3	1	9	8	2	5	7	6
5	4	6	2	1	8	7	9	3
1	2	8	3	9	7	6	4	5
9	7	3	6	4	5	2	8	1
2	1	5	8	6	4	9	3	7
6	9	7	1	2	3	8	5	4
3	8	4	7	5	9	1	6	2

209

1	5	3	8	6	2	7	4	9
7	2	6	1	9	4	3	8	5
4	8	9	7	3	5	6	1	2
6	7	5	2	1	9	8	3	4
2	3	1	6	4	8	9	5	7
8	9	4	3	5	7	1	2	6
9	4	7	5	8	3	2	6	1
3	6	2	4	7	1	5	9	8
5	1	8	9	2	6	4	7	3

210

2	9	8	3	5	7	6	4	1
3	5	7	6	4	1	2	8	9
4	6	1	2	9	8	5	7	3
1	2	6	8	7	3	9	5	4
7	4	3	9	2	5	1	6	8
9	8	5	1	6	4	7	3	2
8	3	2	5	1	6	4	9	7
6	1	4	7	8	9	3	2	5
5	7	9	4	3	2	8	1	6

211

4	8	1	3	7	9	6	5	2
6	2	3	4	8	5	1	9	7
7	9	5	6	2	1	8	3	4
8	4	7	1	9	3	5	2	6
5	3	9	2	6	4	7	1	8
2	1	6	8	5	7	3	4	9
9	7	8	5	1	2	4	6	3
3	5	2	7	4	6	9	8	1
1	6	4	9	3	8	2	7	5

212

6	3	2	4	8	7	5	1	9
8	5	9	2	1	6	7	4	3
7	4	1	5	9	3	2	6	8
9	7	5	3	2	1	6	8	4
1	6	4	9	5	8	3	2	7
3	2	8	7	6	4	9	5	1
2	8	6	1	3	9	4	7	5
5	9	7	8	4	2	1	3	6
4	1	3	6	7	5	8	9	2

213

6	2	7	5	9	4	8	1	3
4	5	8	7	1	3	6	2	9
9	1	3	2	6	8	7	4	5
2	8	9	4	3	1	5	6	7
1	4	6	8	5	7	9	3	2
3	7	5	9	2	6	1	8	4
7	3	4	6	8	9	2	5	1
8	9	2	1	4	5	3	7	6
5	6	1	3	7	2	4	9	8

214

2	3	7	8	9	6	5	1	4
8	5	6	1	3	4	2	9	7
9	4	1	5	2	7	8	3	6
6	2	8	4	5	3	1	7	9
7	9	4	6	8	1	3	5	2
3	1	5	2	7	9	6	4	8
5	7	3	9	6	8	4	2	1
4	8	9	3	1	2	7	6	5
1	6	2	7	4	5	9	8	3

215

7	6	3	8	2	9	4	1	5
1	4	2	3	5	7	8	6	9
8	9	5	6	1	4	7	2	3
6	8	4	2	9	3	1	5	7
5	3	1	7	4	6	2	9	8
2	7	9	1	8	5	6	3	4
9	1	6	4	3	8	5	7	2
3	2	8	5	7	1	9	4	6
4	5	7	9	6	2	3	8	1

216

8	9	6	3	1	4	2	5	7
1	7	5	8	6	2	9	3	4
2	3	4	5	7	9	1	8	6
3	6	1	2	9	5	7	4	8
7	8	9	6	4	1	5	2	3
5	4	2	7	8	3	6	1	9
6	5	8	1	3	7	4	9	2
9	2	3	4	5	6	8	7	1
4	1	7	9	2	8	3	6	5

217

2	5	7	3	9	1	6	8	4
3	4	9	6	5	8	2	1	7
1	8	6	4	2	7	9	5	3
7	6	2	9	1	4	8	3	5
9	1	5	8	6	3	4	7	2
4	3	8	2	7	5	1	6	9
8	2	1	7	3	9	5	4	6
6	7	4	5	8	2	3	9	1
5	9	3	1	4	6	7	2	8

218

9	4	8	7	2	3	1	5	6
3	2	6	5	4	1	7	8	9
1	7	5	8	6	9	4	2	3
6	9	7	1	3	5	8	4	2
2	5	3	9	8	4	6	7	1
4	8	1	2	7	6	9	3	5
8	3	9	4	1	2	5	6	7
7	1	2	6	5	8	3	9	4
5	6	4	3	9	7	2	1	8

219

3	1	4	6	7	8	2	9	5
7	5	8	9	4	2	1	6	3
9	6	2	3	5	1	7	8	4
8	2	3	1	9	5	6	4	7
4	9	6	2	3	7	8	5	1
5	7	1	4	8	6	9	3	2
1	3	5	7	6	9	4	2	8
2	8	9	5	1	4	3	7	6
6	4	7	8	2	3	5	1	9

220

8	1	7	9	4	6	3	5	2
2	6	5	3	8	1	7	9	4
9	4	3	2	7	5	6	8	1
3	7	2	8	9	4	5	1	6
4	9	1	6	5	3	8	2	7
5	8	6	7	1	2	4	3	9
7	2	4	5	3	9	1	6	8
1	5	9	4	6	8	2	7	3
6	3	8	1	2	7	9	4	5

221

6	2	3	1	4	8	9	5	7
1	4	7	2	5	9	8	3	6
5	9	8	3	7	6	1	4	2
9	6	2	8	3	5	4	7	1
7	1	4	6	9	2	3	8	5
3	8	5	7	1	4	6	2	9
2	3	6	5	8	1	7	9	4
8	5	9	4	6	7	2	1	3
4	7	1	9	2	3	5	6	8

222

5	8	1	6	9	2	4	3	7
2	9	6	4	3	7	1	8	5
4	7	3	5	1	8	9	2	6
3	4	7	9	8	5	6	1	2
6	2	8	1	7	4	3	5	9
1	5	9	3	2	6	7	4	8
7	1	4	8	5	9	2	6	3
9	3	5	2	6	1	8	7	4
8	6	2	7	4	3	5	9	1

223

5	2	6	4	1	3	8	9	7
4	7	3	8	9	5	2	1	6
8	9	1	6	2	7	3	5	4
3	1	2	7	4	8	9	6	5
9	8	5	3	6	1	4	7	2
6	4	7	9	5	2	1	8	3
7	3	4	1	8	6	5	2	9
1	5	9	2	7	4	6	3	8
2	6	8	5	3	9	7	4	1

224

5	7	9	3	6	8	4	1	2
1	8	6	7	2	4	5	9	3
4	3	2	9	5	1	7	6	8
3	5	7	1	4	9	8	2	6
9	2	4	6	8	5	1	3	7
6	1	8	2	7	3	9	4	5
8	9	3	5	1	6	2	7	4
7	6	5	4	9	2	3	8	1
2	4	1	8	3	7	6	5	9

225

7	5	1	6	8	3	9	2	4
2	9	6	1	4	7	8	3	5
3	4	8	9	5	2	1	6	7
4	1	9	2	7	5	6	8	3
6	3	5	8	1	9	7	4	2
8	7	2	4	3	6	5	9	1
5	8	4	3	9	1	2	7	6
1	2	3	7	6	8	4	5	9
9	6	7	5	2	4	3	1	8

226

2	3	6	7	1	8	5	9	4
8	4	5	3	6	9	2	1	7
7	9	1	5	4	2	8	3	6
5	2	7	4	8	1	9	6	3
3	6	8	2	9	7	1	4	5
9	1	4	6	3	5	7	2	8
1	5	3	8	2	4	6	7	9
6	8	9	1	7	3	4	5	2
4	7	2	9	5	6	3	8	1

227

3	5	2	8	4	1	9	6	7
1	4	6	5	9	7	3	2	8
7	9	8	6	3	2	4	5	1
5	7	4	2	6	9	1	8	3
8	3	9	4	1	5	6	7	2
2	6	1	3	7	8	5	9	4
9	2	3	1	8	6	7	4	5
6	1	5	7	2	4	8	3	9
4	8	7	9	5	3	2	1	6

228

9	1	2	7	3	4	5	8	6
7	3	5	2	8	6	1	9	4
4	6	8	1	9	5	7	3	2
6	5	4	9	1	2	3	7	8
2	8	9	6	7	3	4	5	1
3	7	1	4	5	8	2	6	9
1	4	7	5	6	9	8	2	3
5	9	3	8	2	1	6	4	7
8	2	6	3	4	7	9	1	5

229

6	7	2	5	1	8	9	4	3
8	1	3	9	6	4	2	7	5
4	9	5	2	7	3	8	6	1
7	4	9	1	3	2	6	5	8
3	8	6	7	5	9	4	1	2
5	2	1	8	4	6	3	9	7
2	6	7	4	8	5	1	3	9
9	5	4	3	2	1	7	8	6
1	3	8	6	9	7	5	2	4

230

1	3	6	5	2	9	8	4	7
2	5	9	8	7	4	3	6	1
7	4	8	3	6	1	2	5	9
9	6	7	1	5	8	4	3	2
8	1	5	4	3	2	9	7	6
3	2	4	7	9	6	5	1	8
5	8	1	2	4	7	6	9	3
4	9	2	6	1	3	7	8	5
6	7	3	9	8	5	1	2	4

231

2	3	9	6	1	5	8	7	4
8	4	5	9	7	3	2	1	6
6	7	1	4	2	8	3	5	9
3	1	8	2	5	4	9	6	7
9	5	2	1	6	7	4	8	3
7	6	4	3	8	9	1	2	5
1	8	3	7	4	6	5	9	2
5	9	7	8	3	2	6	4	1
4	2	6	5	9	1	7	3	8

232

1	5	3	4	2	6	8	7	9
4	7	6	9	3	8	5	1	2
9	8	2	5	1	7	6	4	3
2	3	7	8	4	1	9	6	5
6	4	1	3	5	9	7	2	8
8	9	5	6	7	2	4	3	1
3	6	8	2	9	4	1	5	7
5	1	4	7	8	3	2	9	6
7	2	9	1	6	5	3	8	4

233

9	2	6	8	1	5	7	3	4
5	4	3	7	9	6	8	1	2
8	7	1	4	3	2	5	6	9
6	1	5	2	4	8	3	9	7
3	9	7	6	5	1	4	2	8
2	8	4	9	7	3	1	5	6
1	6	9	3	8	7	2	4	5
7	5	2	1	6	4	9	8	3
4	3	8	5	2	9	6	7	1

234

6	3	9	8	7	1	5	4	2
7	2	4	3	9	5	8	6	1
5	8	1	2	4	6	9	7	3
2	9	8	6	3	7	1	5	4
3	7	5	1	8	4	2	9	6
4	1	6	9	5	2	7	3	8
9	6	2	7	1	3	4	8	5
1	4	7	5	6	8	3	2	9
8	5	3	4	2	9	6	1	7

235

3	6	7	1	2	8	9	4	5
9	2	1	7	5	4	6	3	8
5	8	4	9	6	3	1	7	2
2	7	3	6	1	5	4	8	9
1	9	8	2	4	7	3	5	6
6	4	5	8	3	9	2	1	7
8	5	2	3	9	1	7	6	4
7	1	6	4	8	2	5	9	3
4	3	9	5	7	6	8	2	1

236

8	3	7	5	6	1	4	9	2
2	5	1	3	9	4	7	8	6
9	4	6	2	8	7	3	1	5
1	9	4	7	5	6	2	3	8
6	7	3	8	1	2	5	4	9
5	2	8	9	4	3	1	6	7
3	8	5	4	7	9	6	2	1
4	1	9	6	2	5	8	7	3
7	6	2	1	3	8	9	5	4

237

1	8	6	3	5	4	2	7	9
7	4	3	1	2	9	6	5	8
5	9	2	6	8	7	1	4	3
8	6	9	2	3	5	4	1	7
4	2	1	8	7	6	3	9	5
3	7	5	4	9	1	8	2	6
9	3	8	5	1	2	7	6	4
2	5	4	7	6	8	9	3	1
6	1	7	9	4	3	5	8	2

238

3	5	4	8	7	1	2	9	6
2	6	9	5	4	3	8	1	7
8	7	1	6	9	2	5	4	3
1	8	2	9	5	7	6	3	4
6	3	5	4	1	8	7	2	9
9	4	7	2	3	6	1	5	8
4	2	6	3	8	5	9	7	1
7	9	8	1	2	4	3	6	5
5	1	3	7	6	9	4	8	2

239

4	1	8	7	6	2	3	9	5
3	9	6	4	8	5	2	7	1
7	2	5	1	9	3	6	8	4
9	4	7	3	1	6	5	2	8
2	6	3	5	4	8	7	1	9
5	8	1	2	7	9	4	3	6
8	5	4	9	3	7	1	6	2
6	7	2	8	5	1	9	4	3
1	3	9	6	2	4	8	5	7

240

3	5	2	8	7	6	4	1	9
4	6	1	5	9	2	3	8	7
9	7	8	3	4	1	2	5	6
1	9	3	2	6	5	7	4	8
8	2	5	7	3	4	9	6	1
6	4	7	1	8	9	5	2	3
7	8	4	6	2	3	1	9	5
2	1	6	9	5	7	8	3	4
5	3	9	4	1	8	6	7	2

Puzzle 241

9	8	7	3	1	2	6	4	5
2	1	3	5	6	4	7	8	9
5	6	4	9	7	8	2	3	1
6	4	9	7	2	5	3	1	8
1	2	5	8	3	6	9	7	4
7	3	8	1	4	9	5	2	6
8	9	2	4	5	7	1	6	3
4	7	1	6	9	3	8	5	2
3	5	6	2	8	1	4	9	7

Puzzle 242

8	4	3	2	6	5	1	7	9
2	9	5	7	1	3	6	8	4
6	1	7	9	4	8	5	3	2
5	7	2	3	9	6	8	4	1
1	3	4	5	8	2	7	9	6
9	8	6	1	7	4	2	5	3
4	6	9	8	2	7	3	1	5
7	5	1	6	3	9	4	2	8
3	2	8	4	5	1	9	6	7

Puzzle 243

7	9	6	5	8	4	1	3	2
4	1	2	9	3	7	6	5	8
5	3	8	1	2	6	4	9	7
2	8	3	7	4	1	5	6	9
6	4	1	2	5	9	8	7	3
9	5	7	3	6	8	2	4	1
1	6	4	8	9	3	7	2	5
3	7	5	6	1	2	9	8	4
8	2	9	4	7	5	3	1	6

Puzzle 244

6	2	5	7	1	4	3	8	9
9	1	7	8	3	6	2	4	5
8	4	3	5	9	2	6	1	7
1	9	8	3	4	7	5	2	6
3	7	2	1	6	5	8	9	4
5	6	4	9	2	8	1	7	3
2	5	1	4	7	3	9	6	8
7	3	9	6	8	1	4	5	2
4	8	6	2	5	9	7	3	1

Puzzle 245

1	7	9	6	8	3	5	4	2
4	8	5	2	1	9	7	6	3
6	2	3	4	7	5	1	8	9
9	3	4	7	6	1	2	5	8
5	1	8	3	2	4	6	9	7
7	6	2	5	9	8	3	1	4
3	5	6	9	4	2	8	7	1
2	4	1	8	5	7	9	3	6
8	9	7	1	3	6	4	2	5

Puzzle 246

4	6	2	3	9	7	1	8	5
9	7	8	2	1	5	4	6	3
5	1	3	6	4	8	9	7	2
6	4	5	1	8	9	2	3	7
2	9	1	5	7	3	6	4	8
3	8	7	4	2	6	5	9	1
8	2	6	9	3	1	7	5	4
1	3	9	7	5	4	8	2	6
7	5	4	8	6	2	3	1	9

Puzzle 247

1	8	5	9	4	2	3	7	6
6	7	2	1	3	8	5	4	9
9	3	4	6	5	7	2	1	8
8	2	3	5	7	9	4	6	1
7	6	9	4	1	3	8	2	5
4	5	1	2	8	6	7	9	3
2	1	7	8	6	5	9	3	4
5	9	6	3	2	4	1	8	7
3	4	8	7	9	1	6	5	2

Puzzle 248

9	3	4	2	1	7	6	5	8
6	7	5	8	4	9	1	2	3
8	1	2	3	6	5	4	9	7
1	5	6	7	3	4	9	8	2
2	9	3	1	8	6	7	4	5
4	8	7	5	9	2	3	6	1
3	4	8	9	2	1	5	7	6
7	6	1	4	5	8	2	3	9
5	2	9	6	7	3	8	1	4

249

3	7	9	8	4	5	2	6	1
1	6	4	3	7	2	9	5	8
2	5	8	6	1	9	3	4	7
7	9	1	4	3	8	5	2	6
6	3	2	7	5	1	4	8	9
8	4	5	9	2	6	7	1	3
4	8	6	5	9	7	1	3	2
9	2	3	1	8	4	6	7	5
5	1	7	2	6	3	8	9	4

250

9	8	1	6	5	7	3	4	2
6	2	7	1	4	3	8	5	9
4	5	3	2	8	9	6	7	1
1	6	2	7	3	4	9	8	5
5	4	9	8	2	1	7	3	6
7	3	8	9	6	5	2	1	4
3	1	6	5	7	2	4	9	8
2	7	5	4	9	8	1	6	3
8	9	4	3	1	6	5	2	7

251

2	1	5	4	8	3	9	6	7
9	4	3	1	6	7	2	8	5
7	6	8	2	9	5	1	3	4
1	7	6	8	4	2	3	5	9
8	3	9	7	5	6	4	1	2
5	2	4	3	1	9	6	7	8
4	5	2	6	3	8	7	9	1
3	8	7	9	2	1	5	4	6
6	9	1	5	7	4	8	2	3

252

5	3	8	4	6	7	9	1	2
4	2	9	5	8	1	7	6	3
6	7	1	9	3	2	8	5	4
3	6	4	8	2	5	1	9	7
8	5	2	7	1	9	4	3	6
1	9	7	3	4	6	2	8	5
2	1	3	6	9	4	5	7	8
7	4	6	1	5	8	3	2	9
9	8	5	2	7	3	6	4	1

253

4	3	7	6	1	8	2	9	5
1	8	9	2	5	3	7	6	4
5	6	2	7	9	4	1	8	3
6	1	4	9	8	5	3	7	2
7	9	3	4	2	1	8	5	6
8	2	5	3	7	6	4	1	9
2	7	6	1	4	9	5	3	8
3	5	1	8	6	2	9	4	7
9	4	8	5	3	7	6	2	1

254

2	6	8	4	1	3	7	5	9
5	1	3	7	6	9	8	4	2
4	7	9	8	2	5	1	6	3
8	9	1	3	4	2	5	7	6
7	2	4	6	5	1	3	9	8
3	5	6	9	7	8	4	2	1
9	3	2	5	8	4	6	1	7
6	8	5	1	9	7	2	3	4
1	4	7	2	3	6	9	8	5

255

2	4	9	5	8	1	7	6	3
6	8	7	9	2	3	1	5	4
5	1	3	7	4	6	8	9	2
8	7	4	6	3	5	2	1	9
1	9	6	2	7	4	5	3	8
3	2	5	1	9	8	4	7	6
4	6	1	8	5	9	3	2	7
7	5	8	3	6	2	9	4	1
9	3	2	4	1	7	6	8	5

256

1	4	6	2	8	9	7	3	5
2	7	9	6	5	3	4	1	8
8	3	5	1	7	4	9	6	2
4	1	3	9	6	5	2	8	7
6	5	7	4	2	8	1	9	3
9	8	2	3	1	7	5	4	6
3	2	8	5	9	1	6	7	4
7	6	1	8	4	2	3	5	9
5	9	4	7	3	6	8	2	1

257

6	3	2	7	1	8	4	9	5
5	1	9	3	4	6	2	7	8
7	4	8	2	9	5	3	6	1
1	7	5	8	3	9	6	4	2
9	8	6	5	2	4	1	3	7
3	2	4	1	6	7	5	8	9
4	6	7	9	5	2	8	1	3
2	9	1	4	8	3	7	5	6
8	5	3	6	7	1	9	2	4

258

8	1	4	5	9	3	2	7	6
9	3	7	1	2	6	8	4	5
6	5	2	7	8	4	3	9	1
5	8	1	3	4	2	9	6	7
3	4	6	9	1	7	5	8	2
7	2	9	6	5	8	4	1	3
1	7	8	2	3	9	6	5	4
2	9	5	4	6	1	7	3	8
4	6	3	8	7	5	1	2	9

259

7	3	1	4	2	9	8	6	5
8	6	2	5	7	3	1	4	9
4	5	9	6	1	8	3	2	7
2	8	7	3	6	5	9	1	4
9	4	6	7	8	1	5	3	2
3	1	5	2	9	4	7	8	6
1	2	8	9	5	6	4	7	3
6	9	3	1	4	7	2	5	8
5	7	4	8	3	2	6	9	1

260

2	8	4	3	6	1	7	9	5
7	6	3	8	5	9	2	1	4
9	1	5	2	7	4	3	6	8
6	4	8	7	3	2	1	5	9
5	9	2	6	1	8	4	3	7
3	7	1	4	9	5	8	2	6
8	3	7	9	2	6	5	4	1
4	5	9	1	8	3	6	7	2
1	2	6	5	4	7	9	8	3

261

3	8	6	5	1	4	2	9	7
2	7	1	3	6	9	5	8	4
5	4	9	2	7	8	3	6	1
8	6	5	9	3	7	4	1	2
1	3	2	4	5	6	9	7	8
7	9	4	1	8	2	6	5	3
9	2	8	6	4	1	7	3	5
4	5	7	8	9	3	1	2	6
6	1	3	7	2	5	8	4	9

262

8	6	4	3	9	7	5	2	1
9	5	3	8	2	1	6	4	7
2	7	1	6	4	5	8	3	9
5	1	2	4	3	9	7	6	8
3	9	7	5	8	6	4	1	2
6	4	8	7	1	2	3	9	5
4	2	6	1	5	8	9	7	3
1	3	5	9	7	4	2	8	6
7	8	9	2	6	3	1	5	4

263

4	1	3	5	6	8	7	9	2
7	5	2	1	9	4	6	3	8
6	9	8	7	3	2	5	1	4
2	4	9	8	7	1	3	5	6
8	7	5	6	4	3	1	2	9
3	6	1	9	2	5	4	8	7
1	3	4	2	8	7	9	6	5
5	8	6	4	1	9	2	7	3
9	2	7	3	5	6	8	4	1

264

8	6	3	5	1	4	2	7	9
7	2	4	9	6	3	1	5	8
9	1	5	7	2	8	6	3	4
6	8	9	1	7	5	3	4	2
4	5	7	3	9	2	8	1	6
1	3	2	8	4	6	5	9	7
5	7	8	6	3	9	4	2	1
3	4	1	2	8	7	9	6	5
2	9	6	4	5	1	7	8	3

265

4	8	6	1	5	7	2	9	3
3	1	7	2	8	9	4	6	5
5	9	2	3	6	4	7	8	1
7	4	8	9	3	2	5	1	6
1	6	9	4	7	5	8	3	2
2	3	5	8	1	6	9	7	4
8	2	3	5	9	1	6	4	7
6	5	1	7	4	8	3	2	9
9	7	4	6	2	3	1	5	8

266

6	4	7	5	1	3	9	8	2
9	1	2	4	6	8	7	3	5
5	8	3	7	9	2	6	4	1
4	3	5	1	8	7	2	9	6
8	9	1	2	3	6	4	5	7
7	2	6	9	4	5	3	1	8
2	5	8	3	7	4	1	6	9
3	7	9	6	5	1	8	2	4
1	6	4	8	2	9	5	7	3

267

5	3	8	1	4	7	6	9	2
2	4	7	9	3	6	5	8	1
1	6	9	5	2	8	7	3	4
8	7	3	6	9	4	2	1	5
9	1	2	7	8	5	4	6	3
6	5	4	2	1	3	8	7	9
7	9	1	8	5	2	3	4	6
4	2	6	3	7	9	1	5	8
3	8	5	4	6	1	9	2	7

268

7	8	2	3	6	4	5	9	1
9	6	3	8	5	1	4	2	7
5	1	4	2	9	7	3	6	8
8	9	1	5	3	6	7	4	2
3	4	5	1	7	2	6	8	9
6	2	7	9	4	8	1	3	5
2	5	9	6	1	3	8	7	4
4	3	8	7	2	5	9	1	6
1	7	6	4	8	9	2	5	3

269

5	6	2	1	3	4	8	9	7
4	3	9	5	8	7	1	6	2
7	1	8	2	9	6	4	5	3
3	8	1	4	5	2	9	7	6
2	9	5	7	6	8	3	1	4
6	7	4	9	1	3	2	8	5
9	4	3	8	7	5	6	2	1
1	5	6	3	2	9	7	4	8
8	2	7	6	4	1	5	3	9

270

2	8	5	9	6	1	7	3	4
3	1	7	8	4	5	6	9	2
9	4	6	7	2	3	8	1	5
8	3	1	5	9	2	4	7	6
5	9	2	6	7	4	1	8	3
7	6	4	3	1	8	5	2	9
4	2	3	1	8	6	9	5	7
6	7	8	2	5	9	3	4	1
1	5	9	4	3	7	2	6	8

271

2	6	5	1	7	8	4	9	3
8	1	3	2	9	4	6	7	5
9	4	7	3	5	6	2	1	8
7	9	1	5	2	3	8	4	6
5	3	6	8	4	7	1	2	9
4	2	8	9	6	1	3	5	7
3	8	9	7	1	2	5	6	4
6	5	2	4	8	9	7	3	1
1	7	4	6	3	5	9	8	2

272

5	1	6	7	9	4	3	8	2
9	7	2	6	3	8	5	1	4
8	3	4	1	5	2	9	6	7
6	2	1	3	8	5	4	7	9
4	8	5	9	1	7	6	2	3
3	9	7	4	2	6	8	5	1
7	4	8	2	6	9	1	3	5
2	5	3	8	4	1	7	9	6
1	6	9	5	7	3	2	4	8

273

6	3	9	1	7	4	8	5	2
7	5	8	9	6	2	3	1	4
4	2	1	8	3	5	7	6	9
5	4	3	2	1	8	9	7	6
1	6	2	4	9	7	5	3	8
8	9	7	6	5	3	4	2	1
9	1	5	3	8	6	2	4	7
2	7	6	5	4	9	1	8	3
3	8	4	7	2	1	6	9	5

274

5	7	3	2	6	9	8	1	4
9	6	8	3	4	1	5	2	7
1	2	4	7	8	5	9	3	6
4	8	5	6	3	2	7	9	1
7	9	2	4	1	8	3	6	5
6	3	1	5	9	7	2	4	8
2	1	7	9	5	6	4	8	3
8	4	9	1	7	3	6	5	2
3	5	6	8	2	4	1	7	9

275

1	3	4	7	6	5	8	2	9
9	6	7	4	2	8	5	3	1
2	5	8	3	9	1	4	6	7
7	4	2	1	3	6	9	8	5
6	1	9	8	5	2	7	4	3
3	8	5	9	7	4	2	1	6
5	9	1	2	8	3	6	7	4
8	7	3	6	4	9	1	5	2
4	2	6	5	1	7	3	9	8

276

6	2	5	7	1	8	4	9	3
1	9	7	5	3	4	2	6	8
8	4	3	2	9	6	7	5	1
3	5	1	4	2	9	8	7	6
7	6	4	3	8	1	9	2	5
9	8	2	6	5	7	3	1	4
5	7	9	8	6	3	1	4	2
2	1	8	9	4	5	6	3	7
4	3	6	1	7	2	5	8	9

277

3	1	4	6	5	2	9	7	8
7	9	2	1	8	3	4	6	5
8	6	5	7	4	9	1	2	3
5	2	9	8	7	1	3	4	6
4	3	8	2	9	6	5	1	7
6	7	1	4	3	5	8	9	2
9	5	7	3	6	4	2	8	1
2	4	6	5	1	8	7	3	9
1	8	3	9	2	7	6	5	4

278

9	6	7	5	2	8	1	3	4
5	2	3	9	4	1	8	7	6
8	4	1	6	3	7	5	9	2
1	5	2	7	8	6	9	4	3
7	9	8	3	5	4	6	2	1
4	3	6	2	1	9	7	5	8
3	8	4	1	7	5	2	6	9
6	1	5	4	9	2	3	8	7
2	7	9	8	6	3	4	1	5

279

5	2	8	1	3	9	7	4	6
4	7	1	6	2	5	8	9	3
3	6	9	4	8	7	5	2	1
8	9	2	7	1	6	4	3	5
6	5	7	2	4	3	1	8	9
1	3	4	9	5	8	2	6	7
9	1	5	8	6	2	3	7	4
2	4	6	3	7	1	9	5	8
7	8	3	5	9	4	6	1	2

280

3	7	9	8	5	6	1	2	4
8	5	1	2	7	4	9	6	3
6	2	4	3	9	1	7	8	5
4	9	6	7	1	2	5	3	8
7	8	5	6	4	3	2	9	1
2	1	3	5	8	9	6	4	7
9	6	8	1	3	5	4	7	2
5	3	2	4	6	7	8	1	9
1	4	7	9	2	8	3	5	6

281

1	5	8	4	9	6	7	3	2
4	7	9	2	8	3	1	6	5
2	6	3	1	7	5	9	8	4
5	8	6	3	4	7	2	1	9
9	2	7	5	6	1	3	4	8
3	4	1	9	2	8	6	5	7
7	9	5	6	1	4	8	2	3
6	3	2	8	5	9	4	7	1
8	1	4	7	3	2	5	9	6

282

8	7	4	1	2	6	9	3	5
3	5	6	7	8	9	4	1	2
9	1	2	5	3	4	7	8	6
5	4	9	6	1	3	8	2	7
2	8	7	9	4	5	3	6	1
1	6	3	2	7	8	5	4	9
7	2	8	3	9	1	6	5	4
4	9	5	8	6	2	1	7	3
6	3	1	4	5	7	2	9	8

283

5	8	9	3	1	6	4	2	7
2	1	7	8	4	5	3	6	9
4	6	3	9	7	2	5	8	1
7	3	4	5	6	1	8	9	2
1	5	6	2	9	8	7	3	4
8	9	2	7	3	4	1	5	6
9	7	1	6	5	3	2	4	8
3	4	8	1	2	9	6	7	5
6	2	5	4	8	7	9	1	3

284

5	3	1	2	4	7	8	9	6
9	6	8	5	1	3	2	7	4
7	4	2	8	6	9	5	1	3
8	7	9	3	5	6	4	2	1
1	2	4	7	9	8	6	3	5
6	5	3	1	2	4	7	8	9
3	1	6	4	7	2	9	5	8
2	9	5	6	8	1	3	4	7
4	8	7	9	3	5	1	6	2

285

7	6	3	1	4	8	5	9	2
9	5	2	7	3	6	4	8	1
8	4	1	9	5	2	6	3	7
6	2	5	4	8	9	1	7	3
3	7	4	5	2	1	8	6	9
1	9	8	6	7	3	2	5	4
5	8	9	2	1	7	3	4	6
2	3	7	8	6	4	9	1	5
4	1	6	3	9	5	7	2	8

286

8	2	9	4	7	3	6	5	1
1	6	4	8	2	5	7	9	3
5	7	3	6	9	1	8	2	4
4	9	6	2	3	7	5	1	8
7	8	1	9	5	6	4	3	2
3	5	2	1	8	4	9	6	7
6	4	5	3	1	8	2	7	9
9	1	7	5	4	2	3	8	6
2	3	8	7	6	9	1	4	5

287

8	5	3	4	2	7	6	9	1
1	9	2	6	8	3	7	5	4
4	7	6	1	5	9	2	8	3
2	1	7	8	4	5	9	3	6
6	3	5	2	9	1	4	7	8
9	8	4	7	3	6	1	2	5
7	4	8	5	1	2	3	6	9
5	2	9	3	6	4	8	1	7
3	6	1	9	7	8	5	4	2

288

5	6	4	2	7	3	9	1	8
2	9	7	5	8	1	3	4	6
8	1	3	6	9	4	2	5	7
9	2	8	4	5	6	1	7	3
6	4	5	1	3	7	8	2	9
3	7	1	8	2	9	4	6	5
7	8	6	9	4	2	5	3	1
4	3	9	7	1	5	6	8	2
1	5	2	3	6	8	7	9	4

7	6	8	2	9	4	3	1	5
3	9	5	8	6	1	2	7	4
2	4	1	7	5	3	6	9	8
6	2	4	3	1	8	7	5	9
5	8	7	6	2	9	4	3	1
1	3	9	4	7	5	8	2	6
9	7	6	5	4	2	1	8	3
8	5	2	1	3	6	9	4	7
4	1	3	9	8	7	5	6	2

2	7	8	3	5	6	1	4	9
6	9	3	1	8	4	2	7	5
4	1	5	7	9	2	8	6	3
1	5	4	6	2	7	9	3	8
9	8	2	5	4	3	6	1	7
7	3	6	9	1	8	4	5	2
5	4	7	8	6	9	3	2	1
8	6	1	2	3	5	7	9	4
3	2	9	4	7	1	5	8	6

4	7	2	5	6	9	3	8	1
1	5	6	8	7	3	4	9	2
8	3	9	4	2	1	7	6	5
2	6	1	9	4	5	8	3	7
9	8	5	7	3	2	1	4	6
3	4	7	6	1	8	2	5	9
5	9	3	1	8	7	6	2	4
7	2	4	3	5	6	9	1	8
6	1	8	2	9	4	5	7	3

3	1	4	9	5	7	2	6	8
7	8	6	2	3	1	4	5	9
5	9	2	4	6	8	1	7	3
1	2	3	8	7	9	6	4	5
4	7	9	6	2	5	3	8	1
6	5	8	3	1	4	9	2	7
2	4	1	5	8	3	7	9	6
9	3	5	7	4	6	8	1	2
8	6	7	1	9	2	5	3	4

9	7	1	4	5	3	6	8	2
2	4	6	7	1	8	9	3	5
5	3	8	6	9	2	1	7	4
6	8	3	9	2	1	4	5	7
1	5	7	8	6	4	3	2	9
4	2	9	5	3	7	8	6	1
8	6	4	2	7	9	5	1	3
3	9	2	1	8	5	7	4	6
7	1	5	3	4	6	2	9	8

9	1	4	7	2	3	6	5	8
3	6	5	8	4	9	7	2	1
7	2	8	5	6	1	9	3	4
5	9	6	2	7	4	8	1	3
1	7	2	6	3	8	4	9	5
4	8	3	1	9	5	2	6	7
8	3	9	4	1	2	5	7	6
6	5	1	9	8	7	3	4	2
2	4	7	3	5	6	1	8	9

2	7	8	5	9	1	4	6	3
5	9	1	4	6	3	7	8	2
3	6	4	2	7	8	9	5	1
7	4	6	9	5	2	1	3	8
9	3	5	8	1	6	2	7	4
1	8	2	3	4	7	5	9	6
6	2	7	1	3	5	8	4	9
8	5	9	6	2	4	3	1	7
4	1	3	7	8	9	6	2	5

5	9	2	1	3	8	7	6	4
3	4	8	5	7	6	2	9	1
6	7	1	2	9	4	8	3	5
1	6	4	9	2	7	3	5	8
8	5	7	4	6	3	1	2	9
2	3	9	8	5	1	4	7	6
4	2	3	6	8	9	5	1	7
7	8	6	3	1	5	9	4	2
9	1	5	7	4	2	6	8	3

297

6	7	2	4	3	5	1	8	9
9	5	3	7	8	1	2	6	4
8	4	1	6	9	2	3	5	7
4	9	6	2	7	8	5	3	1
3	2	5	9	1	6	7	4	8
7	1	8	3	5	4	9	2	6
2	8	7	1	4	3	6	9	5
1	6	4	5	2	9	8	7	3
5	3	9	8	6	7	4	1	2

298

9	4	5	3	7	2	1	6	8
2	7	6	5	1	8	4	3	9
8	3	1	4	9	6	2	5	7
1	2	3	9	6	4	7	8	5
5	8	4	7	3	1	9	2	6
6	9	7	8	2	5	3	4	1
3	1	2	6	5	7	8	9	4
4	6	9	1	8	3	5	7	2
7	5	8	2	4	9	6	1	3

299

7	3	8	6	4	1	9	5	2
5	6	2	8	3	9	1	7	4
4	1	9	5	7	2	6	3	8
9	2	5	4	8	7	3	1	6
6	8	3	9	1	5	4	2	7
1	4	7	2	6	3	8	9	5
3	9	4	7	2	6	5	8	1
2	5	6	1	9	8	7	4	3
8	7	1	3	5	4	2	6	9

300

7	3	5	6	8	4	9	1	2
9	1	8	5	2	7	3	6	4
4	6	2	9	1	3	8	7	5
6	2	7	8	9	5	1	4	3
3	5	1	7	4	2	6	9	8
8	4	9	3	6	1	5	2	7
2	8	3	1	7	6	4	5	9
1	9	4	2	5	8	7	3	6
5	7	6	4	3	9	2	8	1